PRAISE FOR *CRAZY FOR THE STORM*
BY NORMAN OLLESTAD

"An elegant memoir as well as a transformative coming-of-age tale. When he leaves his father's limp body behind on the icy plateau—giving it a final kiss and caress as it's claimed by the snow—Ollestad takes his first perilous steps not just into survival, but into adulthood." — *New York Post*

"Cinematic and personal. . . . Ollestad's insights into growing up in a broken home and adolescence in southern California are as engrossing as the story of his trip down the mountain." — *Chicago Tribune*

"Riveting." — *Entertainment Weekly*

"Breathtaking. . . . A portrait of a father's consuming love for his son, *Crazy for the Storm* will keep you up late into the night." — *Washington Post Book World*

"Tragic and exotic . . . [with] short, punchy chapters and . . . nonstop emphasis on adrenaline-fueled excitement." — Janet Maslin, *New York Times*

"Never a dull moment. . . . Ollestad's prose is crisp and exacting, a controlled approach to his tumultuous past. . . . There's enough drama in the plane crash alone to sustain a novel, but Ollestad has done something much more. He's written a beautiful story about a thrill-loving father—'the man with the sunshine in his eyes'—who taught his boy not just how to live, but how to thrive."   — *Houston Chronicle*

"We know Ollestad lived, since he's telling the story, and dramatic as his descent is, the true underbelly of this memoir is the back story—the relationship between Norman and his father. And it is just as compelling as watching a child trying to climb down from an ice-capped mountain."   — *Cleveland Plain Dealer*

"The memoir is as much about a father-son relationship as it is a survival story. . . . Ollestad says his father's life philosophy about surfing and skiing—'knowing there's always a place to go and find peace, clear your mind'—got him down the mountain and through life."   — *USA Today*

"If *Crazy for the Storm* were only about surviving a plane crash, it would be an interesting, intense read. The work is enriched by its structure, chapters that alternate between the experiences on the mountain and Ollestad's memories of childhood. . . . [Ollestad's experience] made him a determined survivor with a writer's gift for teaching through story."   — *Denver Post*

"A page-turning adventure tale . . . and a meditation on manhood."   — *Los Angeles Magazine*

"This is a heart-stopping story beautifully told, an eleven-year-old boy's story that deals with profound and challenging moral and philosophical issues. . . . When does the quest for ecstasy become a danger-junkie's kick? How does a good boy become a good man? How do you raise a child in a busted-up family? Norman Ollestad has written a book that may well be read for generations. It's a book that fathers should give to their sons, but sons should give it to their fathers, too. And mothers, wives, sisters and daughters—read it and weep for all the boys and men you have ever loved." — Russell Banks

"At times beautiful, at times heart-wrenching, *Crazy for the Storm* is a commanding read—a tale that proves the power of the human spirit can rise against any challenge, and a father's legacy can be more than he imagines. — *BookPage*

"An engrossing story of adventure, survival, and psychological exploration. Ollestad hits several notes that should make his memoir irresistible to those looking for page-turning but thought-provoking summer reading along the lines of Jon Krakauer's *Into Thin Air* (1997). . . . Ollestad presents a captivating account of high-altitude disaster that nicely dovetails with his coming-of-age story in '70s California. Deep and resonant." — *Kirkus Reviews*

"The narrative hits a compelling stride midstory when the threads of connection between a father's sportsmanlike hounding of his child become the obvious towrope by which the son navigates later disaster. The structure itself unfolds like a postgame analysis, in chapters that ricochet between the crash site and a Sunday-night highlight reel of father/son athletic adventures." — *The Oregonian* (Portland)

"*Crazy for the Storm* is an absolutely compelling book, which I read in one long sitting. The fact that it's true made me shudder, but then Norman Ollestad is a fine writer and every detail is convincing." — *Jim Harrison*

"In a spare, brisk prose, Ollestad tells the tragic story of the pivotal event of his life, an airplane crash into the side of a mountain that cost three lives, including his father's, in 1979. . . . Although the narrative core of the memoir remains the horrifying plane crackup into the San Gabriel Mountains, its warm, complex soul is conveyed by the loving relationship between the former FBI agent father and his son, affectionately called the "Boy Wonder," during the golden childhood years spent in wild, freewheeling Malibu and Mexico in the late 1970s. Ollestad's unyielding concentration on the themes of courage, love, and endurance seep into every character portrait, every scene, making this book an inspiring, fascinating read."

— *Publishers Weekly*

"I could not stop reading this thrilling memoir. Why do we sometimes feel most alive when we are risking our lives? Ollestad answers this question with a heart-stopping adventure that ends in tragedy and in triumph, a love story that fearlessly explores the bond between a father and son and what it means to lead a life without limits." — Susan Cheever

"Extraordinary—an adventure story with a rich psychological foundation from an enormously talented author. *Crazy for the Storm* is a powerful book. It deserves to be a bestseller."

— Pulitzer Prize–winner Lucinda Franks,
author of *My Father's Secret War*

"As much a thriller as a memoir. . . . Gorgeously written, perfectly controlled." — Carolyn See

"Ollestad's story provides a better blueprint for survival [than Robert Sabbag's *Down around Midnight*] in the purely physical sense. Growing up, he was chased by his father into surfing waves that were too big for him, skiing treacherous mountain chutes, and once ducking bullets in Mexico. While he sometimes resented the education—Little Norm just wanted to ride his bike with his friends and eat birthday cake—he now understands that what he learned saved his life. His journey down the mountain proved the grand lesson of his existence: 'There is more to life than just surviving it,' he writes, and the story ends with Ollestad pushing his own six-year-old son into carving powder in a snowy bowl."   — *Esquire*

CRAZY
for the
STORM

CRAZY
for the
STORM

A MEMOIR OF SURVIVAL

NORMAN OLLESTAD

HARPER ● PERENNIAL

This memoir tells the true story of my childhood, based on my memories, my interviews with family and friends, and my research. Some names have been changed.

Published by Harper Perrnial, an imprint of HarperCollins Publishers Ltd.

First published in Canada in a hardcover edition by HarperCollins Publishers Ltd: 2009
This HarperPerennial trade paperback edition: 2010

HarperCollins books may be purchased for educational, business, or sales promotional use through our Special Markets Department.

HarperCollins Publishers Ltd
2 Bloor Street East, 20th Floor
Toronto, Ontario, Canada
M4W 1A8

Designed by Mary Austin Speaker
Frontispiece photograph © Kramer O'Neill
Map by Paul J. Pugliese
Epigraph photograph courtesy of Norman Ollestad
All other photographs courtesy of Norman Ollestad

Library and Archives Canada Cataloguing in Publication
Ollestad, Norman
Crazy for the storm : a memoir of survival / Norman Ollestad.
Includes bibliographical references.
ISBN 978-1-55468-486-1

1. Ollestad, Norman—Childhood and youth. 2. Ollestad, Norman–family. 3. Ollestad, Norman, 1935–1979. 4. Aircraft accident victims–California–Biography. 5. Aircraft accidents–California–San Gabriel Mountains. 6. Child surfers–California–Biography. 7. Downhill ski racing–United States—Biography. 8. Fathers and sons–United States. 9. Fathers–Death. 10. Competition (Psychology). I. Title.

TL553.9.O46 2010   979.4′053092   C2010-900802-2

Printed and bound in the United States
RRD 9 8 7 6 5 4 3 2

My father craved the weightless glide. He chased hurricanes and blizzards to touch the bliss of riding mighty waves and deep powder snow. An insatiable spirit, he was crazy for the storm. And it saved my life. This book is for my father and for my son.

On my dad's back, Topanga Beach, 1968

I am harnessed in a canvas papoose strapped to my dad's back. It's my first birthday. I peer over his shoulder as we glide the sea. Sun glare and blue ripple together. The surfboard rail engraves the arcing wave and spits of sun-flecked ocean tumble over his toes. I can fly.

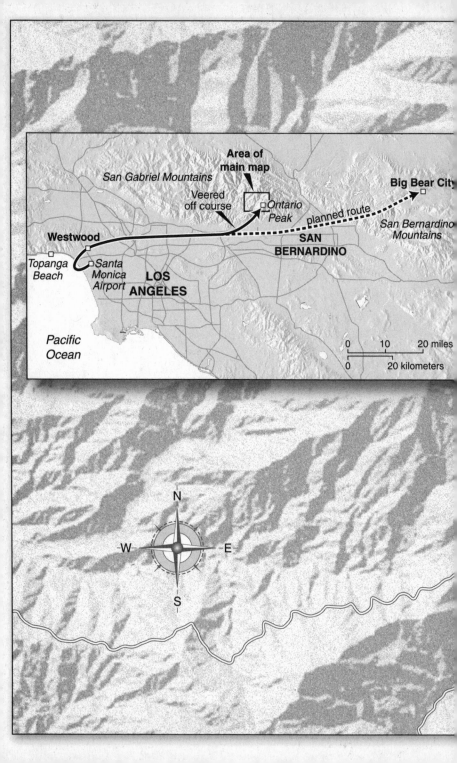

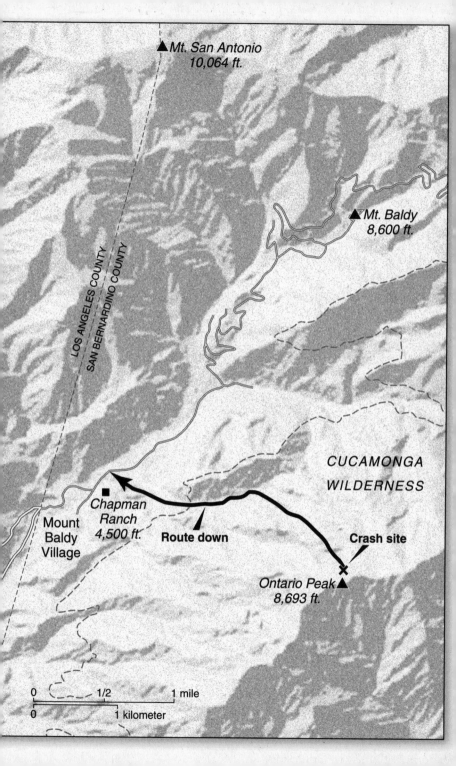

▲ Mt. San Antonio
10,064 ft.

▲ Mt. Baldy
8,600 ft.

LOS ANGELES COUNTY
SAN BERNARDINO COUNTY

CUCAMONGA

WILDERNESS

■ Chapman
Ranch
4,500 ft.

Mount
Baldy
Village

Route down

Crash site

Ontario Peak ▲
8,693 ft.

0   1/2   1 mile

0   1 kilometer

CRAZY
for the
STORM

CHAPTER 1

EBRUARY 19, 1979. At seven that morning my dad, his girlfriend Sandra and I took off from Santa Monica Airport headed for the mountains of Big Bear. I had won the Southern California Slalom Skiing Championship the day before and that afternoon we drove back to Santa Monica for my hockey game. To avoid another round-trip in the car my dad had chartered a plane back to Big Bear so that I could collect my trophy and train with the ski team. My dad was forty-three. Sandra was thirty. I was eleven.

The Cessna 172 lifted and banked over Venice Beach then climbed over a cluster of buildings in Westwood and headed east. I sat in the front, headphones and all, next to pilot Rob Arnold. Rob fingered the knobs along the instrument panel that curved toward the cockpit's ceiling. Intermittently, he rolled a large vertical dial next to his knee, the trim wheel, and the plane rocked like a seesaw before leveling off. Out the windshield, way in the distance, a dome of gray clouds covered the San Bernardino Mountains, the tops alone poking through. It was flat desert all around the cluster of peaks, and the peaks stood out of the desert as high as 10,000 feet.

I was feeling especially daring because I had just won the slalom championship and I thought about the big chutes carved into those peaks—concave slides, dropping from the top of the peaks down the faces of the mountains like deep wrinkles. I wondered if they were *skiable*.

Behind Rob sat my dad. He read the sports section and whistled a Willie Nelson tune that I'd heard him play on his guitar many times. I craned around to see behind my seat. Sandra was brushing out her silky dark brown hair. She's dressed kind of fancy, I thought.

How long, Dad? I said.

He peered over the top of the newspaper.

About thirty minutes, Boy Wonder, he said. We might get a look at your championship run as we come around Mount Baldy.

Then he stuffed an apple in his mouth and folded the newspaper into a rectangle. He would fold the Racing Form the same way, watermelon dripping off his chin on one of those late August days down at the Del Mar track *where the surf meets the turf*. We'd leave Malibu early in the morning and drive sixty miles south to ride a few peelers off the point at Swami's, named for the ashram crowning the headland. If there was a long lull in the waves Dad would fold his legs up on his board and sit lotus, pretending to meditate, embarrassing me in front of the other surfers. Around noon we'd head to Solana Beach, which was across the Coast Highway from the track. We'd hide our boards under the small wood bridge because they wouldn't fit inside Dad's '65 Porsche, then we'd cross the highway and railroad tracks to watch the horses get saddled. When they came into the walking ring Dad would throw me on his shoulders and hand up a fistful of peanuts for lunch. Pick a horse, Boy Wonder, he'd say. Without hesitation he'd bet my horse to win. Once a long shot named Scooby Doo won by a nose and Dad gave me a hundred-dollar bill to spend however I wanted.

The mountaintops appeared higher than the plane. I stretched my neck to see over the plane's dashboard, clasping the oversized headphones. As we approached the foothills I heard Burbank Control pass our plane onto Pomona Control. Pilot Rob told Pomona that he preferred not to go above 7,500 feet because of low freezing levels. Then a private plane radioed in, warning against flying into the Big Bear area without the proper instruments.

Did you copy that? said the control tower.

Roger, said pilot Rob.

The nose of the plane pierced the first tier of the once distant storm. A gray mist enveloped us. The cabin felt compressed with noise and we jiggled and lurched. Rob put both hands on the steering wheel, shaped like a giant W. There was no way we were going to get to see my championship run through these clouds, I thought. Not even the slopes of Baldy where my dad and I had snagged a couple great powder days last year.

Then the gravity of the other pilot's warning interrupted my daydream.

I looked back at my dad. He gobbled down the apple core, smacking his lips with satisfaction. His sparkling blue eyes and hearty smile calmed my anxiety about the warning. His face beamed with pride for me. Winning that championship was evidence that all our hard work had finally paid off, that anything is possible, like Dad always said.

Over his shoulder a crooked limb flashed by the window. A tree? Way up here? No way. Then the world turned back to gray. It was just a trick of light.

Dad studied me. His gaze seemed to suspend us as if we didn't need the plane—two winged men cruising a blue sky. I was about to ask how much longer it would be.

A bristle of pine needles streaked past the window behind him. A shock of green, clawing open the mist. It was snowing now. Then a spiky limb lunged at the window. An evil ugly thing that Dad was unaware of. It sucked all life from the cabin, scorching the scene like a photograph eaten by fire. Suddenly my dad's face was blotched and deformed.

Time seemed to decelerate as if lassoed by a giant rubber band. Fog pressed against all the windows and there was no up or down, no depth at all, as if the plane were standing still, a toy hanging from a string. The pilot reached down with one hand and spun the knee-high trim wheel. I wanted him to spin the dial faster—we'll climb faster, away from the trees. But he abandoned the trim wheel and steered the giant W with both hands, jerking us side to side. What about that dial? Should I spin it for him? A branch out the window caught my eye.

Watch out! I yelled, curling my four-foot-nine, seventy-five-pound body up tight.

The wing clipped a tree, sending a thud into my spine, and the plane twisted ass-backwards. We bounced like a pinball off two more trees—metal ripping, the engine revving. I was fixated on the trim wheel. Too late to spin it now. . . .

We slammed into Ontario Peak, 8,693 feet high. The plane broke apart, flinging chunks of debris across the rugged north face and hurling our bodies into an icy chute.

We were sprawled amongst the wreckage. Our bodies teetered on the 45-degree pitch threatening to plunge us into an unknown freefall. Exposed to freezing snow and wind, we dangled 250 feet from the top—the distance between life and death.

CHAPTER 2

THE SUMMER BEFORE the crash my grandmother's washing machine broke. Grandma and Grandpa Ollestad had retired to Puerto Vallarta, Mexico, and the inflated prices for appliances in Guadalajara or Mexico City would have strained their budget. Also, renting a truck and picking up a new machine themselves was a major ordeal in those days. So my dad decided he would go to Sears, buy a new washer and haul it down to Vallarta himself. He would borrow Cousin Denis's black Ford pickup, cross the border in San Diego and cruise the Baja Peninsula highway all the way to La Paz. He'd take the ferry across the Sea of Cortez to Mazatlán, which was mainland Mexico, then head farther south through the deep jungles, hitting as many of the rumored surf spots as he could before reaching Vallarta.

Hearing this news made me stiffen with fear. I went silent when my mom explained it all to me on our way home from summer school, where she taught second grade and I was preparing for sixth. She didn't say anything about me having to go but it was in the air—looming—more threatening than if it were a certainty. The idea of baking inside that pickup truck for three or four days and hunting for surf—and worse, finding it and having to paddle out in big waves and float alone out there with just my dad in the vast sea—was not appealing at all. He would be focused on the surf and I would be left to fend for myself. I envisioned my body crushing under the lip of a wave, tossing around, clawing upward, gagging for air.

Mom's car turned onto the Pacific Coast Highway and I heard the ocean shushing. I was staring at my blue Vans, listening to the Beatles on the eight-track, and I felt carsick and had to look out the window.

We arrived at my mom's house on Topanga Beach, the southernmost cove in Malibu. The homes were built right on the sand, slapdashed together and teetering at all angles as if shelter were an afterthought, second to the essential need of being on the beach. My dad used to live there also. When I was three he moved across the highway into a cabin on the edge of Topanga Canyon. By the time I was ten I had gathered various tidbits of information, forming a sketchy portrait of what broke up my parents.

Mom complained that sometimes the phone would ring in the middle of the night and Dad would leave without a word and return with no explanation. Mom knew it had to do with Grandpa Ollestad or Uncle Joe, my dad's half brother, who always needed Dad to save their ass, but Dad wouldn't talk about it. When Mom protested her exclusion from certain family secrets, my dad just shrugged it off. He would go surfing or simply walk away if my mom persisted. The final straw had been when my dad secretly loaned Uncle Joe money from Mom and Dad's joint savings account and then refused to tell my mom why.

Right after this incident a French guy named Jacques came to visit. He was a friend of a friend of Dad's. My dad had just gone through major knee surgery and could barely move around, so he loaned Jacques a surfboard and called out instructions from the porch, using his crutch to guide Jacques to the takeoff spot. Dad didn't have the strength to show Jacques around Malibu, so Mom took him to Point Dume—a chain of pristine coves— and to Alice's restaurant on the pier, and to the Getty Museum. After Jacques went back to France Dad stopped coming home at night. This lasted a couple of weeks. Then he returned for a few days, until he finally moved his stuff into the cabin across the highway.

Mom started hanging out with a guy named Nick. Right from the get-go Nick liked to mix it up, which was the opposite of my dad, who was reluctant to fight with my mom. Nick and Mom had spectacular clashes in front of everyone on the beach. It wasn't that abnormal really—a lot of people on Topanga Beach who were married were kissing other people, fighting with their new boyfriends or girlfriends, and suddenly moving into other houses. It was an incomplete picture of what went wrong between Mom and Dad. Something was obviously broken, that's all I knew, and was forced to accept it.

Mom parked the car in the garage and I immediately found my three-legged golden retriever Sunshine. She was waiting on the outdoor walkway that ran along the side of our house. Sunny and I ran to the porch, jumped over our beach stairs and ambled up the beach to the point—a curve of sand that came to a tip at the north end of the cove.

Two girls my age cantered their horses bareback through the waves washing along the shore. I held Sunny so she wouldn't spook the horses. The girls lived up the canyon in the Rodeo Grounds, below where my dad lived, and as always we just waved to each other. The horses kicked up salt water onto the girls' legs, which shimmered in the late afternoon light.

When they disappeared up the mouth of the canyon I threw Sunny's stick into the surf. A blond dude with a long beard dressed in full Indian garb did a rain dance toward the setting sun. He reminded me of Charles Manson, who was always hanging around the beach when I was a baby, and used to serenade my aunt while she rocked me in her arms on our beach stairs.

Good thing I never went up to that commune he kept talking about, my aunt said when she told me the story.

After dinner I tried to fall asleep to the crashing waves. I read the Hardy Boys to help take my mind off the trip to Mexico. Later I woke and made a tent with my covers and played a spy game, radioing secret information to headquarters via the rusted posts of my old brass bed. Sunshine lay curled at the foot of the bed and guarded our hideout. I petted her and told her about how I hated having to surf, hating not being able to play all weekend like the kids in the Pacific Palisades.

I often complained to my dad about not living in a neighborhood. He told me that one day I'd realize how lucky I was living right on the beach, and that since Eleanor (my unofficial godmother) lived in the Palisades and I got to stay there sometimes, I was doubly lucky.

But she doesn't have a pool, I said, and Dad rebutted that I had the biggest pool in the world right in my own front yard.

Before I was born my mom used to work at Eleanor's nursery school, Hill'n Dale, and my parents became close friends with Eleanor and her husband Lee. I started going to Hill'n Dale when I was three and Eleanor immediately lavished me with attention. We have the same birthday, May 30, she liked to tell everyone. Ever since the first grade I had walked the two blocks from grammar school to Hill'n Dale, hanging out there until my mom or dad picked me up after work. All those years of seeing Eleanor practically every day made me think of her as *my other mother*, and I told people so.

Morning brought good news—my dad had to prepare a malpractice case with his law partner Al before leaving for Mexico so I wouldn't have to surf this weekend, and Sandra would be joining my dad on the trip to Mexico. The odds of not having to go were now heavily in my favor. I was so dizzy with relief that I didn't realize what Nick had in store for me until it was too late. Nick had been living with my mom for several years by now and he talked about *mouthpieces* and *jabs* and said that Charley, the only boy my age still living on the beach, was coming over. I was preoccupied, basking in a heaven devoid of Mexico and teeming with sleepovers and birthday parties and frosted cakes.

The sand was hot and white. It was August and the fog was long gone and the sun beat down. Nick and his friend Mickey drank beer and drew a circle in the sand.

That's the boxing ring, said Nick. Don't step outside the ring or you'll be automatically disqualified.

Everybody said Nick looked like Paul Newman. He was taller than my dad and didn't have broad shoulders—I had decided it was because he didn't surf. He was different from my dad in a lot of other ways too. He would never dance at parties like my dad always did. And Nick didn't play any instruments like my dad, or sing—stuff Dad learned to do when he was a child actor. Dad was in the classic *Cheaper by the Dozen*, acting in several films and TV shows through his early twenties. On a show called *Sky King* Dad played a mechanic, which was funny because he couldn't fix anything, not even my bike. And I couldn't imagine Nick running a summer cheerleading camp like my dad did. That's how Dad met my mom—he was recruiting *song girls* to teach at his camp and my mom was staying with one of the song girls in an apartment in Westwood by UCLA. It was 1962. Dad had just resigned from the FBI and was working as an assistant U.S. attorney under Robert Kennedy. He and his friend Bob Barrow, who grew up near Dad in South Los Angeles, cooked up the idea of organizing a summer cheerleading camp as a way to make some extra money and meet college girls. Dad would teach the girls dance routines in the mornings before suiting up and going into the Department of Justice.

On their first date Dad took my mom to Topanga Beach. He played guitar for her and convinced her to paddle out surfing with him. They got married a year later, moving into a house on the beach.

Mickey helped Charley and me string up our boxing gloves. Mine had been acquired in a trade for my Raggedy Ann doll with a boy who was moving from the beach. This went down following a particularly tyrannical evening with Nick after which I had announced my desire to learn how to box. Then a few days later, as if to show that he was unfazed by my sudden urge to box—an obvious gesture meant to protest Nick's drunken rages—Nick put together this little bout between Charley and me.

It'll be good for you, Norman, he said.

While Mickey secured the knots Charley and I craned our necks to peek around the flat-topped dirt knoll on the point.

Stop leering at the naked ladies and put your mouthpieces in, said Nick.

The nude beach was just around the dirt knoll and both Charley and I quickly denied any interest in girls.

Good, said Nick. You know what's behind those tits and asses?

Charley and I looked up at Nick, waiting with our eyes and ears wide open.

Mothers and grandmothers and brothers and sisters and cousins that you have to deal with, he said. Weddings and anniversary parties. Endless headaches.

Charley and I waited for more, but that was it.

You'll get it one day, said Nick. Mouthpieces in?

Yeah, I said.

Good. Your mom would have a complete nervous breakdown if you lost your teeth.

Mickey was chugging down his beer. He looked back into the cove at my house where my mom was watering plants on the deck.

Okay, said Nick. Keep your hands up and keep your feet moving.

Like Muhammad Ali, I said.

Nick smiled and I could smell the beer on his breath.

Yeah, just like Ali.

Charley didn't look nervous at all. He was two inches taller and about ten pounds heavier. We circled each other and I danced like Ali. I saw some openings between Charley's glove and shoulder, enough room to punch him in the jaw, except my arm just lurched instead of shooting forward to punch him. Again, I tried to swing but my muscles tightened and I had to break through their resistance to throw a punch that ended up as a fly swat across Charley's forehead. Then all of a sudden he came at me. I put my hands up and he hit me in the stomach and I lost my breath and turned sideways and he hit me in the nose. A stinger went down my body to my feet. It wasn't as simple as pain. It was liquid and it was cool like the ethyl alcohol that my dad used to wash out his ears after surfing. My eyes watered and instantly I was scared shitless. I looked around for help and Nick was squinting at me, lips pursed.

Ready to quit? he said.

I nodded. Charley threw up his arms in victory.

I put out my hands for Nick to unlace my gloves and he rubbed his forehead and sighed and put down his beer. Charley moved with a confident swagger and Mickey complimented him on his toughness, and that brought to mind my crying over my Raggedy Ann doll the night after I made the trade. I had wanted it back. It was the only toy left from when my parents lived in the same house'. But it was too late—the boy and my doll were already in another city.

Charley got his gloves off first and said he was going skateboarding with Trafton and Shane and a few of the other legends on the beach. They were going up to Coastline where the pavement was new and the streets were wide and steep and rolled on forever.

Your mom specifically forbids that, Norman, interrupted Nick before I could make my plea to tag along with Charley.

I looked at him and I felt my face turn red and my chin quiver.

It's too dangerous, he added.

I touched my nose and it was sore and he seemed pleased that it didn't make sense—allowing me to box but not go skateboarding.

Life is a long series of readjustments, he said, patting me on the back as if to soften the unfairness. Better to get used to it now, Norman, he added.

Nick and Mickey went ahead of us, carrying the gloves and mouthpieces so that we wouldn't lose them. I followed Charley to his house near the point.

You can come along if you want to, he said.

I didn't need his approval, I knew all those guys too, but I pretended to be grateful.

CHAPTER 3

N EAR THE TOP of Ontario Peak I woke up. Feathers rocked from the sky and coated my face. I had been dreaming but could not remember the dream. Were Dad and I just gliding side by side down a powder run?

Wind rustled through the spruce needles, so pure and uncluttered that I wondered if I was still asleep. I was kinked over and a section of the instrument panel crossed the foreground. One corner of the panel sunk into fog like an upended ship. A few feet beyond it was a big tree trunk. It crossed the other way, making an X with the panel. It was impossible to know where the horizon line was and my eyes strained to orient myself. Then the fog thinned like a flock of birds lifting and one of the airplane wings was stuck into the tree trunk. All these weird mashed-together pictures did not add up to anything that made sense. Chaotic swirls of snow fell sideways and back upward then disappeared behind a whitewash of incoming fog.

I tried to breathe but couldn't get enough air into my lungs. My stomach was choked off by my seat belt, which strapped me into the seat. I called for my dad.

I can't breathe, I bellowed. Dad I can't breathe!

Pinned on my side by my seat, I couldn't turn around to check on my dad and Sandra in the back. I went in and out of consciousness—like sinking into a murk of water and then suddenly rising to the top only to drop into the murk again. The whole thing is just a nightmare, I decided. A nonsense dream. Can't wake up though.

I noticed something beyond the shattered cockpit—the pilot seemed sprawled out as if diving backward and there appeared to be a bloody cavity where his nose should have been. A reef of fog swallowed him before I could be sure.

I tried to breathe again. Just a speck of oxygen. My hand fumbled for the seat belt buckle and my blue mid-top Vans squeaked against the snow. The buckle released and my lungs burned with cold air. Dad will fix this, I told myself. He'll turn everything right side up again.

I felt myself winding down, an engine sputtering. My head was light, eyes blurry. I had no idea where I was. Eyes began to close and I surrendered.

CHAPTER 4

WHEN CHARLEY AND I loaded into the VW bus it was filled with smoke from the joints going around. I took a puff, careful not to inhale too deep, and Big Fowler had to jump out so that the bus could make it up the beach access road to the Coast Highway. A mile south we turned off the highway past the Getty Museum. Shane floored it so we could climb to the top of the hill, then one of the girls would drive the bus down to where Coastline crossed another street and went uphill—the run-out.

Barefoot and shirtless, hair in ponytails, the gang spilled out of the sliding bus door. Polyurethane wheels were fairly new, replacing the old clay ones, and I was awed by the swooping high-speed S-turns the gang carved down the center of the street. Charley and I watched until the succession of dangled arms disappeared around the first bend.

All that remained was the black slope. Charley didn't seem

intimidated and stepped right onto his board and took off. I had never skated anything this steep and I didn't want to be all alone up there. I rolled forward, kept my turns long and made sure to curve back up the hill before starting the next turn. Charley went around the bend in a tuck and I worried that he would finish way before me and that everyone would be watching as I dribbled in last.

I sucked up my fear and pointed my board down the center of the street. In an instant I was flying. As I came around the bend I could feel the board start to wobble. I shot out of the turn and kept leaning up into the hill, trying to eat up some of the speed. The wheels sent violent quivers into the trucks—the metal axle below the skateboard deck—and up through the deck into my legs and my legs vibrated like loose exhaust pipes. Hold on, I told myself. The sidewalk was closing in and I had to start the next turn. I fought the whipping motion and shifted my weight to my toes and suddenly the wheels stuck and the board booted me into the air. I landed on my left hip, bouncing twice before my skin gripped the pavement and refused to let go. I put my hand down and my elbow came with it, flipping me over. When I finally stopped my back and ass were scraped raw too.

The air stung the whole left side of my body and the ground hurt against my backside. My hand burned and my hip throbbed but all I cared about was if anybody had seen me eat it. I looked up—Charley was already around the next turn.

My skateboard was in a rosebush and I plucked it out, scratching up my other hand. I threw down the board and pushed off, making big round turns for the remaining quarter mile. When I reached the run-out Charley was sitting against the bus with all the guys and the girls with the flowers in their hair.

What happened? said Charley.

Looks like Norm wiped out, said Trafton.

I nodded and pulled my trunks off my hip to show them my war wound. It was as red as a raspberry and bloody and the skin surrounding it was smeared black.

Check out that road tattoo, said Shane.

Everybody laughed and my bravado shrank.

You must've been hauling fucking ass, said Trafton.

I shrugged.

Way to shred, said Trafton.

Thanks, I said.

I didn't have to look at Charley or anybody else—I knew I had their respect now. I pulled up my trunks and picked up my board. Charley offered me a sip of beer and I said no.

My mom was standing outside our garage, so Shane pulled the bus over at the top of the access road and I slipped out amongst a group of boys and right through someone's gate. The gang climbed back into the bus and I heard it sputter away. I hoped nobody was home because I didn't really know these people too well, only that a boy who visited one weekend a month stayed here with his father. I decided to walk down the stairs around the side of the house in order to make my way back home via the beach.

The stairs dropped past a window and I saw the boy's father below on a bed. He was between a woman's legs fucking her. I stared straight down on them and the woman turned her head side to side and her cheeks were pink and when she moaned a ripple of excitement washed down the center of my body. I could never share this with Dad. He'd tease me if he knew I liked girls. So would all his friends.

The boy's father thrust hard into the woman and she cried out and I couldn't take my eyes off her. Then he rested down on top of her. My nose was inches from the glass and the glass was steamed up from my breath. I stepped back from the window and there was a wet spot on it the size of my face.

I dreamed about her pink cheeks as I wandered down by the mossy rocks exposed at low tide. To the south near the bottom of the cove Bob Barrow, Beer-Can Larry, and Nick's brother Vincent were hunched around the poker table on Barrow's porch. I heard some scratchy noises next to me and turned. Music echoed from the yellow house where all the best surfers lived. They called that house the yellow submarine. Nick used to live there before he moved in with my mom. I was shocked when I found out that he didn't surf. Trafton and Clyde appeared on the upper deck with their electric guitars. They stood stiff-legged and rehearsed bluesy riffs.

A woman with crow-black hair drifted down the beach as if carried by the wind. She fluttered to the foot of the yellow house and lay on the sandbank formed by the waves at high tide. She gazed up at Clyde and Trafton stroking their guitars. I ambled off the rocks onto the wet sand, drawn to her. She rolled onto her back and looked out at the ocean and bobbed her head to the jam. I kneeled down and dug a hole in the sand and stole glances up her miniskirt. Her body was magnetic, which seemed natural enough, but I was unsure of what to do with the excitement coursing through me.

At first I didn't notice her watching me. It seemed like a long process of me tearing my eyes away before I noticed her there, looking at me. She studied me as if I had not been looking up her skirt but up some other woman's skirt, detached, like she was studying a photograph of this scene. She didn't seem to care that I was staring at her private area. Like the nude sunbathers around the point didn't care whenever Charley and I meandered up there.

I picked up my skateboard and walked home.

. . .

I scurried over the ivy growing out of the sand in front of our porch. I heard a door slide open and saw my mom step onto the side walkway. It was shaded in there. Her silhouette moved around in the darkness and then went back inside. I made a run for the walkway. Once under it I hid my skateboard on the lower shelf behind the dog and cat food. I walked to the sliding glass door and stepped inside.

My mom's torso was curving out from the laundry room doorway. She leaned back and looked at me.

Where have you been, Norman?

Down the beach.

Without Sunshine? she said.

Sunny came out from under the kitchen table, tail wagging and wiggling as if she hadn't seen me in years. I kneeled down and petted her and kissed her snout.

You're lying, said my mom.

What are you talking about?

You were skateboarding. Your board was gone.

I don't keep it there anymore because Dad keeps dinging the surfboards on it.

I ducked into my room, which was right off the kitchen. I shut the door and Sunny scratched it as I whipped off my T-shirt and put on a long-sleeved shirt.

Coming out of my room I went right to the fridge, drinking from the milk bottle. My mom appeared on the other side of the fridge door.

Are you telling the truth?

Yes.

Don't lie to my face. It makes it worse, Norman.

I'm not lying. Ask the guys. I didn't go.

She eyed me and I shrugged.

Why are you wearing a long-sleeved shirt? she said.

I'm going up the canyon, I said.

She looked confused and sort of worried. I called to Sunny and we crossed through the kitchen into the living room, past Nick's rocking chair from which he watched the news every night. I thought about having to watch the Watergate hearings and Nick shouting at the TV from that rocking chair with a bottle of vodka in his hand.

Sunny led the way, jumping off the step into my mom's sunken bedroom and bounding through the opened sliding glass door onto the porch. Sunny was missing her front left leg but that didn't stop her from leaping off the porch onto the sand.

She knew where we were headed. Topanga Canyon emptied at the point, the creek water gathering into a pond that trickled into the ocean, gushing when the winter rains came. We navigated a dirt pathway around the pond overgrown with licorice plants. The smell perfumed the air. I tore off a limb and chewed on it and tore off another and gave it to Sunny. A VW bus was still in the middle of the pond, having washed down the canyon after a big rain years ago. On a dare I once swam out there and stood on its roof.

Under the bridge it was cooler and the cars rumbled overhead. We came out the other side and the path meandered along the sandy edges of the creek. I led Sunny into the bamboo stalks and we sat down on our tattered blanket within the confines of our fort. I continued to tell Sunny a story I was writing about Murcher Kurcher, the famed detective who was looking for the *Mona Lisa* thief aboard a ship bound for Europe. As I spoke I wrote it down on the pad of paper I kept rolled up in an old metal thermos that I found in the canyon.

At the end of my story I told Sunny that when I got older I'd have big muscles and would kick Nick's ass if he yelled at me or bossed me or my mom around anymore. Sunny looked into my eyes. She always listened like I was the most important person on earth.

CHAPTER 5

*M*Y BODY QUIVERED like a freight train and woke me. I was freezing cold, and the cold defied the soft fog wrapping around me. It was the same as when I woke up the first time—an impossible landscape devoid of shapes, a bottomless cloud that I seemed to tumble through. Then I saw the twisted instrument panel.

I tried to move and I was on my side in my flipped-over seat. The slope, a curtain of ice, dropped from my hip, so steep I wondered why I wasn't sliding down it. Carefully, I turned only my head. My blond hair was stuck to a piece of metal that was torn and jagged like a giant piece of tinfoil. The frozen strands cracked as I turned.

I searched beyond the instrument panel to where the tree had been before. Foamy clouds walled it off. The foam ball washed over me and I lost my sense of up and down again.

Slowly I gained buoyancy like a fetus adapting to its milky

chamber. The experience of skiing in a whiteout flickered across my mind. Ignoring the instrument panel I supposed that maybe I had hit a tree and that Dad couldn't find me in the storm.

The fog undulated, as if breathing, and it lifted off the snow for a moment. Fifteen feet across the slope the pilot's shoes wandered in disparate directions. His legs twisted in the snow. The hem of his shirt folded back and his belly was pale.

Am I still asleep?

I squirmed away from my seat, bumping my foot against the instrument panel. It dropped away, as if through a trapdoor, down the curtain of ice, vanishing in the fog. I wanted off this sheer face and scuttled on my hip and shoulder across the slope. I wondered if the pilot was really as mangled as he had looked. I heard another piece of the plane move, metal scraping ice, but all I could see was fog crawling upward. I was slipping too so I stopped. I rolled onto my stomach. The cold cut right through my ski-racing sweater and Vans. The weather was warm in Big Bear yesterday, I thought. Wish I had my gloves and jacket and ski hat now. I clung to the ice with everything I had: bare fingers, chin, chest, pelvis and knees. The curtain of ice climbed right past my nose into the fog, so steep I seemed on the verge of falling backward. Then fog closed around me, encapsulating me in a tiny gray pod.

I inched across the curtain, from left to right, toward where I had spotted the pilot. A few minutes later the ice softened to a hard crust and it was easier to grip. I noted this change in snow texture, this easier-to-grip section. When I got close I saw the pilot's nose resting on the snow next to his face. The empty cavity was frozen with blood and his eyes strained open as if looking over his forehead. His brains leaked out the back of his skull.

I called for my dad.

Searching the drifts of fog swarming from all directions, I was not able to find him.

Dad. Dad! I called again.

A woman's voice echoed then dwindled away in the wind.

I followed the voice and found Sandra above me, a dim figure veiled in fog. She was still in her seat, torn free of the body of the plane. A blast of snow obliterated her for a moment and when it cleared I could see. I was in a gully that tunneled upward into the high clouds and fog. Dad and I would call it a chute. It ran down from the peak of whatever mountain this was, and I guessed it poured into a wider slope or a canyon below. I looked downward and the concave ice slide reminded me of the Hangman's Hollow run in Mammoth. *Not for the faint of heart*, my dad had said. I assumed jagged rocks, now covered in fog, bordered this chute, as in Hangman's Hollow.

I hope it's a short chute that ends just below that line of fog, I told myself. Not some thousand-footer.

I looked upward again to find Sandra. She was perched just to the right of an even steeper, slicker groove in the chute that ran vertically down this side of the chute. Skiers would call it a funnel. When avalanches broke from the high peak they'd wash down into this funnel, wiping away everything, leaving a polished slick of ice. That's where I had been before I crawled away from my seat—in the funnel. The funnel sucked everything into it like a black hole. Have to stay away from it.

Sandra was crying and trembling.

Your father is dead, she said.

I glanced around and could not find him anywhere. She's just upset, I decided. Need to find him though. Through a fresh wave of mist and wind I searched for my dad. As the mist cleared I looked back toward the funnel section. Dad's figure appeared just above my seat, just above where I was a few minutes ago—the pitch so steep and the fog so thick that I had not seen him there crumpled behind my seat. He was hunched over. The crown of his head pressed against the back of my seat. His face between his knees.

Dad had come forward and across to my side. Did he lunge to protect me, or was he thrown?

What are we going to do, Norman? cried Sandra.

Another surge of fog swept over me, passing quickly, then I saw that Sandra's shoulders were crooked like a wilted puppet. Her hair was tangled around a wound in her forehead and it stuck to the tacky blood clumped there. She kept talking and I turned to study my dad's body again, trying to figure out how he ended up against my seat. His arms were limp resting on his thighs and his hands dangled over his knees.

Oh God, Norman, said Sandra.

He might just be knocked out, I said.

No. No. He's dead.

I refused to accept this. It was impossible. Dad and I were a team, and he was Superman. Sandra wailed and her right shoulder hung too far below her collarbone and I realized that it was dislocated, like she was, and that gave me confidence that she was wrong about my dad. She put her other hand over her face, sobbing like a madwoman.

CHAPTER 6

NICK CAME HOME after dark and my mom served my favorite honey chicken. She ate on the couch and Sunny and I ate on the floor and Nick ate in his rocking chair with a jug of wine. I was feeling clever, having told my mom that the scrape on my arm was from falling on my way up the creek. Her easy acceptance of my story, which seemed airtight, made me feisty for some reason. And after dinner, when Nick insisted on watching a news special about Watergate, I had the nerve to protest.

I want to see what sordid facts they've picked up over the years, said Nick.

Oh Jesus, said my mom. Do we have to?

Fucking-A right we have to.

I leapt up and turned the channel and looked back at Nick.

Turn it back, Norman, or I'll play Chi-cow-ski.

It's Tchaikovsky, said my mom.

Nick's listless expression made it clear that he was not amused by her correction. His curly hair was standing up off his forehead and combined with his tired dull eyes, it made him look slightly derelict.

Turn it back, he said.

No, I said.

He rocked forward and rose out of the chair in one motion. He took a swig of the wine.

Chi-cow-ski!

I ran back to Sunny and slid down behind her. Nick moved Sunny over and straddled me, fastening down my shoulders, and Sunny squirmed on her back and licked his arm and my face. Nick forked his fingers like a mad piano player and jabbed my chest.

Dum dum dum dummm, he sang, his wine-breath making me gag, and I turned my head.

His knees pinched my arm skin and his fingers rammed my chestbone and ribs.

Dum dum dum dummm! Chicowski plays until you promise to change the channel, he said.

Mom, I can't breathe. Tell him to stop!

Nick. He can't breathe. Stop.

Repeat after me, said Nick, still playing.

Okay. Okay.

I will never defy Nick again.

I will never defy Nick again, I said.

He drew his upper body back and his wrists went limp and he stared off into the distance.

Get off so I can change the channel, I said.

Nick looked down over his nose and his eyes focused far beyond as if some apparition could be seen deep in the rug. I wasn't going to wait for him to get up and I twisted away.

My shorts slid off my waist and my raspberried hip caught his attention. His eyes flared open.

I quickly pulled up my shorts, avoiding eye contact, and turned the channel to the Watergate special.

There, I said. Should I do the dishes?

Well that's nice of you, Norman, said my mom.

Then you guys can watch the special, I said.

Nick was still on his knees, arms hanging down, head tilted forward. He didn't turn or move or speak. All I saw was his back inhaling and exhaling. I went to the kitchen and began soaping the dishes. I could hear Nixon and the other bad guys denying they had anything to do with the break-in. Suddenly Nick's voice cut through the TV noise—*skateboarding* was the only word that was clear. Then I heard the investigators talking about what was really going on in the White House at the time—the cover-up. Nick didn't call me into the living room and his voice never cut through the sound of the TV again so I figured I was okay. By the end of the dishes Nixon was giving his Checkers speech and some secret tapes were playing.

Nick lit up a joint and stared at the TV screen with hatred. He took off his shirt. I walked in front of the screen. Watergate Watergate blah blah blah, I said. I'm so sick of Watergate.

Nick blinked as if trying to focus on my foreground image.

You have no fucking idea, he said.

About what? I said.

He rocked out of the chair, suddenly enraged. You know why *you* of all people need to watch this?

My face was even with his bare stomach. The air in the room had changed. It closed in all around me.

I'm going to bed, I said.

As I turned he grabbed my arm and his fingers dug into my bone.

Ouch! I said. You're hurting me.

Damn fucking right. Now answer the question.

What's the question?

Why do *you* of all people need to be watching the downfall of the president of the United States?

I already watched it a couple years ago, I said.

Well you need to watch it again. Do you know why?

No, I said.

Did you hear that, Jan? I bet you don't know why either.

My mom was putting away the chicken. She walked under the archway between the kitchen and the living room and stopped.

Don't know what? she said.

Pay fucking attention. That's the problem. You never pay attention.

My mom put a hand on her hip and looked at Nick. She lifted her eyebrows and sighed. His fingers bore deeper into my bone and the pain made me cry out.

Let go of him, said my mom.

You'd like that, wouldn't you? But you know why I can't? he said, seemingly to both of us.

Why? she said, rolling her eyes.

Because if I let him go now he'll end up like Nixon.

Oh come on, said my mom. What the hell are you going on about?

He's a liar!

I didn't see him skateboarding, she said. Did you?

So you believe him?

She looked at me and I tried to warn her with my eyes but I was still cringing from the pain in my arm.

Yes, she said.

Nick ripped down my pants and the waistline tore the scab and fresh blood percolated to the surface of my wound.

What about this? said Nick, pointing at my raspberry.

Oh God, said my mom. Where did you get that?

I wanted to be on her side. I wanted her to win.

I got it when I slipped in the canyon, I said.

Bullshit, said Nick. Look at the blacktop around the edges.

That's dirt, I said.

Nick rubbed his fingers over the black smudges. Ouch, I said.

Stop that, Nick, said my mom.

He held up his fingers.

It ain't dirt.

Yes it is, I said.

Nick pointed at the TV. You sound just like Nixon, he said. It comes so naturally.

I recalled Nixon's voice, cracked and high-pitched during his Checkers speech. Nixon had a fake smile. A warped frown. No one on the beach liked him. My dad grunted and cast him off with the wave of his hand—not even worth talking about.

Then Nick let go of my arm and I ran into the kitchen.

Come back here, he yelled.

Leave him alone, said my mom.

Get your ass back here, said Nick.

I ducked into the bathroom and peed into the toilet. I heard Nick arguing with my mom about me forgetting to take out the trash cans again, for the second week in a row. It was proof, he said, that *Norman believes the world revolves around him*.

I came out of the bathroom and my mom was face to face with Nick.

You're overreacting, she said to his perspiring face.

Horseshit, he said and marched past her and into the bathroom and I knew I was busted before he even said it.

He forgot to flush the goddamn toilet again, barked Nick. This is at least the tenth time, Jan.

Nick stepped out of the bathroom and called me over. You need to clean the toilet bowl. That's the only way you're going to learn.

My mom stepped between him and me.

Get the fuck out of the way, said Nick, his eyes cutting hard down at my mom. She shook her head, making a stand.

I skulked into the bathroom.

It always starts when you're young, Nick said. You lie a little, cheat a little. And then all of a sudden that's your mentality. That's who you are.

Nick, said my mom. You used to lie your ass off when you were a kid. That's why you got kicked out of grammar schools and high schools and military schools. So don't act like Norman's got the problem, Nick.

Nick slumped against the door jam like an animal backed into a corner. He was a hairline trigger away from exploding. Don't do or say anything Mom, I thought to myself.

She swung her hip out to the opposite side.

You think you're right because you're drunk and stoned, she said. But you're wrong.

The word *wrong* seemed to prod Nick from deep down, and whatever it unleashed crawled up his neck and his veins popped out and the thing continued into his face turning it purple-red and wound his eyes up like a cartoon character. It wasn't funny though, and I stopped breathing.

His jaw set and his front teeth sawed together.

I'm the fucking truth, he said, grinding up the words. And you two are fucking lies.

He stared at me, red-faced, veined and perspiring.

I can't let you grow up to be a liar. A failure. I have to stop it. There must be consequences.

He stepped past me and pulled out a jar of Ajax and a sponge from under the sink and handed them to me.

Scrub the toilet bowl, he said.

I looked at my mom standing in the kitchen with her hand still on her hip. She shook her head, but I was afraid to defy him. I dumped the Ajax into the toilet bowl.

You don't have to, said my mom.

Your mother doesn't care about you, Norman, he said. She wants you to be a liar and a failure. Do you understand that? She's too lazy to stop you.

Shut up, Nick, she said. Norman's not a liar. You are, Nick. You are!

His body tensed as if jolted by electricity.

You know I'm right, he said.

Nick looked down at me. You know I'm right, he repeated.

He may be drunk and stoned, I thought. He may be crazy. But he was right—I had lied.

I held the sponge and Ajax and my mom looked at me, half eclipsed by Nick's stomach. She shook her head. It wasn't clear whether she was signaling for me not to scrub the toilet or whether she was just disgusted with the whole situation, or both.

The hair on his stomach was inches from my face and he smelled like sour milk.

You'll wake up one day and realize the world does not revolve around you and it will be too late, he said. You'll be too old to change. You'll end up bitter and frustrated for the rest of your life. Save yourself, Norman, he said. Because your mother can't.

My mom scoffed. She either didn't know or didn't care that I had lied, and this ambiguity created a void inside me, a space for Nick's demons to take root.

I began scrubbing.

You don't have to do that, said my mom.

He knows I'm right, said Nick.

You're a joke, said my mom.

I kept scrubbing and then I heard Nick's rocking chair creak. I heard my mom march into the living room and they started yelling at each other. I wished I could yell too—better than just shrinking up like a bug.

He called her a cunt. She said he wouldn't know what to do with one if it fell in his lap. Then I heard the sound of meat and bone colliding. A second later a dull thump against the floor. I dropped the sponge and ran into the living room.

My mom was on the floor. She held both hands over one eye. She whimpered like a child, curled and fetal. Nick stood over her. He moved his feet like a nervous horse. I got between Nick and my mom.

You're a bully, I said.

He swallowed and his Adam's apple rose and fell. He turned and went to the freezer. I kneeled down and asked my mom if she was okay.

I'm fine, Norman. You should go to bed now. Everything will be okay. Don't worry, she said. I promise.

I didn't see how things would be okay. I didn't see how that was possible. She was either lying or didn't understand what was really going on.

I'm going to run up to Dad's, I said.

No! she said. Don't do that, Norman.

Why? He'll protect us.

If you try to run away I'll track you down, said Nick. You'll never make it.

He sounded like an actor in a movie. He came through the archway with ice wrapped in a towel. In that moment he looked melodramatic and ridiculous to me. Nick handed the wrapped-up ice to my mom. His blood-veined eyes slanted across his face at me. I turned away and saw the sliding glass door and imagined myself escaping out it. I was running up Topanga Canyon to my dad's house—he would fix everything—but Nick was chasing me on the bridge over the creek and it was dark and his fingers snagged my hair. Feeling myself crash to the ground made my courage wither, exposing something else beneath it, and I stood frozen in the living room, eyeing my escape route, defeated.

In the middle of the night I woke to the cry of a dying animal. I opened my bedroom door and heard my mom moan as if in agony. I stepped toward her room and was about to call out, Are you okay? when she moaned again. It sounded different, as if a note of joy rang out from a frenzy of dark chords, and I realized they were fucking. It dawned on me that their fight had seemed like a show, like they were actors playing parts in a made-up story.

I went back to my bed and thought about how I had lied and about Nick being right and my mom being wrong and about Nick hitting her and how now they were fucking, as if they knew all along that that was how the night was going to end.

CHAPTER 7

S *ANDRA STOPPED CRYING.* Her hand remained over her face. She is wrong, I thought. My dad is for sure still alive. I have to check on him.

I was facing the wrong way in the chute. I had to turn around. A blinding gust scrabbled over me and I closed my eyes, visualizing how I'd make my 180-degree turn. I remembered how Dad had taught me about ice—you always have to keep an edge— and I replayed the time I slipped on the face of Mount Waterman and he dive-bombed the ice face and scooped me up like a shortstop. *Once you get going, Ollestad, it's hard to stop.*

When the flurry passed I reached my downhill arm uphill and tried to grab the snow next to my uphill shoulder. My fingers closed around a feeble top layer of crust, knuckles scuffing the hard pack below. So I stabbed my fingers into the hard pack. One knuckle deep. Enough.

I compressed like a ski racer making a high-speed turn,

poised on the inside edges of my Vans. Then I unweighted and swiveled my hips 180 degrees, crouching right back into my race pose for stability.

I inched across the chute, slanting the edges of my rubber soles into the crust like I would skis. No steel rail to carve into the hard snow, so I compensated with precise balance. As I crossed into the funnel, a subtle dimple—the threshold between the crust and the intractable ice curtain—I was forced onto my stomach again. I clawed, fingernail to fingernail, across the funnel.

Must be getting close to Dad, I thought, and glanced up from the curtain. A pool of fog clung to him and his curly brown hair appeared. There was some silver in it. Blond surfer hairs, he'd say.

I raked both hands deep into the ice. Spikes of pain weakened my fingers, creeping up my arms. Don't look down, I told myself. Then I pulled violently to cross the last few feet to my dad. Snap, I lost my grip and went rifling down the curtain instantly.

Out of habit I yelled for my dad. Searched for him above as I descended. I glimpsed his flaccid hand, a pale shape in the mist. It's not reaching for me.

I twisted like a snake falling down a waterfall, waggling my arms farther out to one side, lunging for anything. I snagged something. My fingers clamped down around it. A spindly evergreen. It bent and I jerked to a stop. I hung on. I got one hand dug into the ice to take pressure off the baby tree, kicked in toe-deep ledges while never letting the other hand unwrap from the needles.

Tears came and I opened my mouth to call for him. Instead I shut my eyes and felt the drops freeze to my cheeks.

I swore at the mountain and at the storm and I cried between outbursts. None of this was helping me—he was still up there drooped over—and my skin stung from the damp cold seeping through my sweater and sneakers. My only option was to try to climb back up by myself.

CHAPTER 8

I HEARD MY DAD'S feet banging the loose wood boards along the side walkway. A part of me woke. A part of me clung to the peaceful cocoon of sleep. He wasn't supposed to be here. He was supposed to be working on his malpractice case with his law partner Al, whom he went into private practice with a few years ago. They were supposed to be helping some poor guy who lost his leg because someone built a crappy bridge that collapsed, something like that.

The sliding door swished open. Dad never knocked when he came to get me early in the morning. I guess he didn't want to wake them up. I burrowed deeper into the promise of Sunday morning—no basketball or football or skiing and certainly no surfing. Nick's going to make his Sunday morning pancakes soaked in maple syrup. It'll be like nothing ever happened. I rehearsed my plea to Dad: I have hockey camp coming up at the end of August. Come on, Dad. Just one day off.

My bedroom door squeaked. Sunny lifted her head from the corner of the bed. Dad's warm palm touched my back. Warm lips on my cheek. I pressed my eyes closed, hoping he would have pity on me—poor tired little boy.

Good morning, Boy Wonder, he said.

I moaned, evoking exhaustion.

Sure is a beautiful day out there, he said.

I whimpered like a child lost in a dream.

Time to get up, he said.

I'm too tired, I said in a strained whisper.

The wind will be up early so now's the time, Ollestad.

I hurt my whole body . . . falling. I scraped up my whole body.

Let me see.

I pushed down the covers and showed him my hip and elbow and hand.

Salt water is the best thing for it.

Oh man. It's gonna sting like hell.

Just for a second. The iodine's good for it. Get up.

My whole body aches, Dad.

Just one good ride, Ollestad. It'll be over before you know it. I'm going to be gone for a week so you get a vacation, he said, smiling.

No, I whined.

As far back as I could remember I was on a surfboard. It wasn't until last summer down in Mexico that Dad got serious about me riding waves as opposed to just farting around, as he called it, in the whitewash.

No, I moaned.

Hey, I didn't get to learn until I was in my twenties, he said. All I had was baseball. You're lucky you get to ski and surf when you're young. You'll be ahead of the game.

I need a day off, I said as I pulled up the covers.

He looked away and it reminded me of how cowboys did that in the movies when they lost patience and were trying to simmer down. His faded red trunks hung under two ridges of muscle sculpting his lower abdomen and his shoulder dimpled when he patted Sunny and told her she was a good dog for helping me get ready to surf. I thought he was going to repeat the story of how he financed his first ski trips in the late '50s: showing Bruce Brown surf films in the town halls of Aspen and Sun Valley. Instead he dropped my beavertail wetsuit on the bed.

Put it on, he said. I'm going to wax up the boards.

We hauled our surfboards toward the point where the pond leaked into the ocean. We passed by yesterday's boxing ring and I remembered getting hit in the nose and then my mom getting hit in the eye. If I told my dad about it, and told him what Nick said to me about running for help, would they get in a fight? I envisioned Nick grabbing a wine bottle and swinging it at my dad, splitting his forehead. I had always sensed that my dad didn't want to know the gory details of my mom's private life, didn't want to get involved. The wine bottle splitting Dad's head and his silent plea not to know joined forces, persuading me to keep my mouth shut.

We paddled side by side until a group of bigger waves, set waves, rose on the horizon. He pushed my board from the tail and told me to paddle harder. We barely made it over the first two swells. The third swell was the biggest and the lip of the wave curled over my head and I punctured through its belly and the lip slapped down on my legs. The salt stung my wounds. When we cleared the rock shelf I sat up. My hip was stinging and the wetsuit pressed the salt water tight against my raw skin.

My dad had previously spoken about *fighting through things to get to the good stuff* or some such concept, and as he shook the salt water out of his curly brown hair, he talked more about people *giving up and missing out on fantastic moments.*

Accordingly I pearled on my first wave, nose-diving and swallowing water, and he told me to keep trying because I'd be so happy once I got a good ride. I snapped back that I hated surfing.

I saw Chris Rohloff paddling out. I had not seen him in a few months. He was two years older than me but we were buddies. His dad lived in the Rodeo Grounds (or Snake Pit) below where my dad lived on the rim of the canyon. We started hanging out after I saw one of his dad's surf movies at the yellow submarine house.

Rohloff tried to catch a few waves but didn't have the strength to get one. So my dad paddled inside and pushed Rohloff into a wave.

He rode the whitewash almost to shore. Rohloff hooted and thrust his arms up and I felt spoiled for not wanting to learn as badly as he did.

When Rohloff paddled back out he was beaming.

Hey Little Norm, he said. Your dad stoked me.

That was a good one, I said.

I'm totally into it.

Me too, I said.

Here's one for Ollestad, said my dad.

He lined me up under the two-foot peak and gave me a little shove. I knew it would be my last one if I didn't wipe out. I focused on each step of the process. I got to my feet, bent my knees, leaned back, then corrected my balance when the board reached the bottom. Being goofy-footed I stood with my back to right-handed breakers, pressing the heel of my left foot into the tail of the board, leaning back toward the wave. The board curved into the pocket. I streaked for thirty yards, bending my knees and weighting forward and backward to control the pitch of my board across the moving wall.

. . .

I came ashore in front of my mom's house. She was watering her plants again and I could see her black eye. I hauled my board to the house. When I got to the ivy I rested.

How was it? she said.

Did you see that last one I got?

Her clear eye fixed on me and the lid batted down a couple of times.

Yes, she said. Good one.

I knew she was lying.

Of course it was a white lie, sweet, yet I was ashamed and the board suddenly felt really heavy going up the porch stairs. Her lie seemed to give Nick the edge in the battle of who would be right about me, and I resented her for it.

Look, said my mom. Norm's on a good one.

My dad's arms hung at his sides like an ape-man. His upper body was quiet as his feet crossed over, walking him to the nose. His toes gripped the edge of the board and skimmed the water. He leaned back, a curved prow. He rode like this to the sand and casually stepped off the board and let it wash up on the sand before scooping it into his arms.

My mom watered with her good side toward him.

Good morning Janisimo, said my dad.

Good wave, Norm, she said.

Little Norman got a beauty too, he said. Did you see it?

She nodded and I cringed. He trotted up the stairs and my mom kept faced away from him and he did a double take on her. I watched him and he didn't seem to notice the bruise. He walked the board to the side walkway and put it up on the shelf. I handed him mine and he put it away.

He leaned down and kissed my cheek and salt water shed off

his mustache and tickled my nose. He looked at me. Chunks of different-colored blue cracked his irises and his cheeks bunched up like rosy apples. He told me he loved me.

I'll be back in a week, he said.

Bye, Dad.

Adios, Boy Ollestad.

He walked back toward the beach. My mom heard him coming and tried to appear busy with some weeds in one of the pots. My dad circled around to her bruised side.

Ah shit, he said.

My mom spoke in a whisper with her back to me. My dad's eyebrows forked down between his eyes, then he looked away like he was pissed off, as if casting the piss into open territory would help disperse it.

My dad appeared to be gathering anger and I liked it, thinking that this was step one in him becoming a force against Nick. A charge of redemption welled up inside me. Then like a reverberation I imagined Nick's red eyes stalking my dad and there was something in Nick's hand, a weapon.

At the end of the shadowed walkway I saw my dad studying me. Something raw lurked deep down in his eyes—a look he got when he rode waves or skied powder. He was looking over my mom's shoulder. She was still talking. He nodded and said something to her before walking toward me. Mom turned with him and her eyes followed Dad down the walkway. Even with a shiner she looked young and innocent gazing at my dad with moist, yearning eyes. Her lips peeled apart and her body leaned toward him. Dad didn't stop or look back. I wondered if that was how he left when he finally moved out for good. Had Mom hoped he really wouldn't leave—that it was just temporary? Jacques had gone back to France and Dad hadn't spent the night at the house for a couple of weeks. He surprised me one evening coming through the sliding glass door in the kitchen after work in a gray suit with a bow tie and wire-rimmed eyeglasses. He limped but didn't use crutches. He read me a bedtime story and once I was asleep he confronted my mom. She was planning on going to Paris to see Jacques.

It's either Jacques or me, my dad said.

She wouldn't answer one way or the other. I refuse to choose, she said. A couple days later Dad moved out.

Mom and Dad kept up their appearances at bridge night for a few weeks, playing as a team against other couples like they had been doing for years. Their friends all held out hope that they would get back together. Jan and Norm were seen as the perfect match.

Mom's eyes blinked a few times, as if tamping something down, and she turned back to the weeds in the pot. I tugged on the string attached to my zipper and began peeling off the wetsuit. I wasn't holding out hope that they would get back together—I had known them as two separate entities far longer than as a couple, so it seemed normal to me.

So, he said when he came astride me.

I looked up at him, brushing my hair out of my eyes. His shoulders were silhouetted and they looked wide and blocky—a powerful image.

Nick's full of shit, Ollestad. Don't listen to him.

I know, I said, thinking Dad never said that to Nick's face. They were always real friendly to each other and there was never any sign of tension. Not even jealousy. At least none that I ever saw.

Steer clear of him, okay? said Dad. That's what I do.

I thought of how I might do that, maneuvering around his body in the living room, eating dinner in my room, playing with Sunny in my fort.

What if he grabs me?

My dad looked away, casting something off again, this time into the muted light. He made a faint growling sound in his chest that I'd heard before.

Don't say anything to Nick, my dad grumbled. Nod your head and just stay out of his path.

I was perplexed, trying to figure out how to do that, and he added,

Stay at Eleanor and Lee's as much as possible while I'm gone.

Dad knew that Eleanor showered me with unconditional love, that she was my fairy godmother. Everyone always said that Eleanor and I had an immediate, inexplicable connection from the moment I was born. And I never passed up a chance to stay with her and get treated like a prince, so I said okay.

I'll call Eleanor when I get home, he said.

I nodded and he looked worried. He put his hand on my shoulder.

I'll be back later, he said. We'll see how you feel in a couple hours. Okay?

I nodded again, not understanding what a couple hours would change.

He moved directly in front of me, reeling me in with his infectious smile.

See you in a couple hours, he said.

Okay, I said.

He took the walkway toward the access road this time, stepped into the sun and vanished.

I spent the rest of the morning at my fort with Sunny. I came home to get some milk because it was hot out. My mom was on the phone and I guzzled half the bottle.

Norman. Wait.

She hung up the phone.

That was your dad.

Yeah.

He wants you to come with him to Grandma and Grandpa's.

I scrunched my face.

It'll be fun, she said. You guys will surf on the way down and the ferry's really neat. And you know Grandma and Grandpa will be thrilled to see you. Besides you get to skip a week of summer school.

There was no accounting for the fact that my fear of surfing in Mexico outweighed my fear of confronting Nick again, even after he had just given my mom a black eye.

I don't want to go, I said.

Well you'll have to talk about it with your father. He wants you over there right now. Let's pack up.

She moved toward my room. Staying put, I rested my hand on Sunny's head.

Norman.

I shook my head.

Why do I have to go?

Because. Because it will be good for everyone. You haven't seen your grandparents since last summer. Don't you miss them?

No.

Well according to your father you're going, so you'll have to work it out with him.

Why? I thought Sandra was going.

Apparently she's not going anymore.

Shit, I said.

CHAPTER 9

I *ASCENDED FROM* the baby tree, trying to veer out of the icy funnel. I reached my right arm as far to the right as possible, anchored my fingertips into the ice and raked my body laterally. I repeated this several times before my fingers gouged crust instead of ice and I knew I was outside the funnel. It took a long time, maybe thirty minutes, to climb the remaining twenty feet to my dad. I wasn't going to slip again. I knew I had gotten lucky nabbing that tree.

I hiked past pilot Rob. His disembodied nose was dusted over and one side of his body was collecting snow, forming a drift. Soon he would just be a lump under the snow. A fact, like the wind and cold, that I filed away, not quite believing.

My dad was only two or three feet above me when I found him. Same position: seated, his upper body doubled over, his wrists bent over his knees.

I put my lips to his ear.

Dad. Wake up. Wake up.

I shook him and that broke my footing. My feet skated for purchase and I had to let go of him for fear of dislodging him and sending the two of us down the ice slide. The snow was softer in this spot and luckily my fingers got a good hold. I decided to dig out a shoe step so that I could attend to him.

While I kicked my shoe toes into the crust Sandra began to jabber—a circle of mixed-up words and phrases. My Vans only blunted against the snow, hammering my toes until the pain forced me to stop. I looked to my right and uphill a few feet. Sandra was still perched on the edge of the funnel. I watched her for a moment. Her eyes drifted, the lids opening and closing in time with her alternating eruptions and low murmurs. Consciously I turned her noise level down and she faded away.

I kicked into the snow again. My feet were numb and stiff now and that helped me hack out a step. Then with my other foot I hacked out another step. I had two secure leverage points. I clamped both hands around my dad's arm and shook him.

Wake up. Dad. Dad. Dad!

Wind spearheaded down the chute and scraps of plane teetered and I heard my seat groan, making me turn my head. Poof, my seat shot down the curtain. Gone in a flash. I let go of my dad, worried again that I might send the two of us down the icy chute.

I rested my palm on my dad's back. He didn't seem to be breathing. What if Sandra's right, I thought. What if he's dead?

I watched the wind-driven snow thrash from all directions, wave after wave. My toes cramped from having to grip the tiny notches in the snow—the only thing keeping me from plunging down like my seat. Another blast of wind nearly tipped me backward and I had to hug close to the ice curtain. Even the trees I saw earlier looked cold and afraid, huddling for protection, I thought.

The wind hushed and I leaned toward my dad again.

Daddy, I said, pressing my palm to his back.

But he was folded in two like a broken table.

He had taught me to ride big waves, had pulled me from tree wells and fished me out of suffocating powder. Now it was my turn to save him.

I wormed my shoe tips deeper into the notches. Got plugged in. With the heels of my palms under his shoulders I pushed. He didn't budge and I was pinned under him like a scrawny stick trying to hold up a big rock. So I got over him and tried to pull him up. Too heavy. If only I was bigger and stronger.

Why am I so small? You're such a weakling.

I stared down at him. My fingers quivered and pain seeped into my heart. His curly hair tickled my nose as I leaned in to kiss him, hugging him tight to my body.

I'll save you. Don't worry, Dad.

He's still warm, I told myself and squeezed him closer.

CHAPTER 10

M Y MOM'S VW Squareback climbed the Topanga Beach access road. The hard gray suitcase rattled in the back. We darted across the Pacific Coast Highway, turned up the canyon, then into my dad's dirt driveway. Suddenly a guy on a motorcycle was coming right at us, a plume of dust around him. My mom slammed on the brakes and the bike swerved around us and I glimpsed Sandra's silky hair. Her arms were around the guy's stomach.

Sandra and I locked eyes for an instant. She looked angry and her mouth tightened.

Hey I don't even want to go, called my inner voice. You go. You go!

Then Sandra was whisked into the dirt cloud.

My God, said my mom. They almost ran right into us.

Where is she going? I said.

I have no idea, she said.

That's how it always was with Sandra, a mystery. She just appeared one day with my dad down at Barrow's and it was understood that she was his new girlfriend. Beer-Can Larry called her a *feisty little honey* and a *dark Scot*. Her skin would tan a dark caramel brown—except for her pink lips, thick compared to her otherwise delicate face—and her wide-set chocolate eyes blended in with her skin when she got really tan. Barrow said he was sure she was from a poor neighborhood in Scotland, even poorer than his and Dad's old neighborhood. After fighting with my dad she would always come shrinking back. Once when they were broken up she came by my dad's office and asked for money, desperate, and he gave her some. He even signed something so that she could extend her visa. He seemed to feel sorry for her, wanting to protect her all the time. Nonetheless Sandra hated that I always came first, her eyes flaring at me when Dad had to take me to hockey practice or away skiing.

When we got in the pickup truck the seats were already sticky. My dad wedged his guitar case behind the seat bench and tuned in a country station that was playing his favorite, Willie Nelson. It was dusk when we hit the Tijuana border. A fat man in a uniform and hat approached us. He circled around the truck bed, eyeing the tarped washing machine and our two surfboards rainbowing over the edge. He waddled to my dad's window.

Buenas nochas, said my dad.

The man nodded and asked in Spanish for something. My dad reached in the glove compartment and handed the man the Sears receipt. The man inspected it for a long time. Then he said a number—I knew this because I had learned some Spanish while visiting my grandparents last summer.

My dad grumbled and said a different number.

The man smiled and flashed his gold teeth. Before the man spoke again my dad handed him some pesos. The man counted them. As he did my dad put the truck in gear and rolled forward. The man looked around before stuffing the money in his pocket, and my dad hit the gas.

Why'd you have to pay him?

They call it a tax. But it's a bribe.

Isn't that against the law?

Sure is. But he is the law.

He's the police?

Basically.

If the police break the law then who arrests them?

I don't know. Good question, Ollestad.

He let me stew over the paradoxes for a while. Then he spoke.

In a poor country like Mexico people try to get money any way they can. They even do it in a rich country like America. It's not right. But sometimes—like with that guy—you play along because you understand the circumstances.

He checked on me a couple of times as we wound out of Tijuana and back along the coast. It was black outside. A few lights scattered around in the distance.

He's a liar then, right? I said.

The border guard?

Yeah.

Uh-huh. That's right.

I wanted to blurt out that I had lied too, about skateboarding, about where I got my scrapes. I pressed my forehead against the passenger's window. I could feel my dad's eyes on my back. I flashed on Nixon, his saggy jowls and hunched shoulders, and the policeman's gold teeth, and him sitting in his box all night and him taking money from people and stuffing it in his pocket.

Take it easy on that window, Ollestad, said my dad.

Sorry.

You want to rest your head in my lap?

Yeah.

I swiveled around and put my cheek across his thigh and my bent knees up on the seat so my feet could fit against the door.

Sunlight poured in the truck's window onto my head. I sat up and wiped my forehead with my T-shirt.

Buenos dias, said my dad.

I noticed the creases under my dad's eyes—they were lined in an olive yellow, standing out against his smooth honey-brown skin. He looked older and more tired than I had ever seen him look. He drank coffee out of a Styrofoam cup.

Where are we? I said.

Just pulling out of Ensenada.

One eye was still blurry and I looked out the windshield. The sun cut across the sagebrush and the sage climbed the hills, spotting them with dull greens. It reminded me of Malibu. I looked west out the passenger's window beyond the bald head-land cliffs, and the Pacific Ocean spread as far as my eye could see, the water tinted peach in the morning light.

My dad yawned.

Did you sleep? I said.

Yeah. I pulled off to the side of the road in Rosarito and took a nap.

Why didn't Sandra come?

His smile drained away like water seeping into sand. He stared out along the highway and his eyes narrowed.

She was pissed off at me about something, Ollestad.

What?

It's complicated.

Did you fight?

Yeah. But that's not why she's mad.

Why's she mad?

Nick's brother. You know Vincent, right?

I nodded.

Yeah well he thought it was funny to take Sandra's bird.

He took her little parrot?

Yeah.

Why?

To play a joke, he said shaking his head.

What kind of joke?

He pretended to be a birdnapper I guess. We even left money in that phone booth by George's Market. We didn't know it was him until he showed up with the bird.

My dad moved his puckered mouth from one side to the other just like Grandpa did sometimes.

Sandra wanted me to call the cops, he said.

Did you?

Naw.

So she left?

Yeah. She gave me an ultimatum.

Like you better or else?

Exactly.

Who was the guy on the motorcycle?

I don't know. Some friend of hers.

His eyes were soft and the hook-shaped bone of his brow was less pronounced. There was no sign of that raw animal in there.

Why didn't you call the cops? I said.

Vincent is a friend of mine.

I had seen my dad and Vincent play poker together at Barrow's house on the beach and I had always thought it was weird that my dad was friendly with my mom's boyfriend's brother. But I didn't say anything about that.

Was what he did against the law?

My dad nodded.

Then why didn't you call the cops?

It was just a stupid prank.

If you were still in the FBI would you have arrested him?

He laughed.

No. We went after real bad guys, not pranksters.

I stared out the window at the road. I had heard about my dad's one-year FBI stint, stationed in Miami from 1960 to 1961. About the book he wrote exposing J. Edgar Hoover's hypocrisies, one of the first of its kind.

Dad joined the FBI at age twenty-five. It was a coveted job, demanding a graduate degree, preferably in law. Before joining he read every book he could find about J. Edgar Hoover, the director of the FBI, wanting to familiarize himself with the man who was considered the greatest crime fighter in American history.

In the first weeks of FBI training school Dad was shocked to find so many cracks in the facade. The instructors boasted to his class that no president would ever fire Hoover and that Congress never dared challenge the great director's assertions about anything. Dad was surprised when he took his first exam and the instructors gave everyone in the class the answers— ensuring the success of Hoover's policy that all FBI agents get A's on the exams. The only real test was the final one, when he met the director himself. Hoover either gave you his blessing or dismissed you as unfit. If you caught his eye then you were thrown out. If he didn't like your physical appearance, such as a pinhead-shaped skull, you were dismissed.

On Dad's first day as an agent he couldn't understand why

all the veteran agents picked the most beat-up FBI cars from the garage, even though they were unreliable in a chase and the radios didn't work. He learned that Hoover's policy stated that if any agent damaged an FBI vehicle in any way, even in a chase, he would have to pay for it out of his own pocket. Hoover's policy kept insurance costs way down and allowed Hoover to brag to the congressional Ways and Means Committee that he was saving tens of thousands in taxpayer dollars. A few weeks later Dad realized that Hoover was assigning a disproportionate amount of agents to finding stolen cars. He figured out that Hoover did this to inflate the FBI's statistics, counting retrieved stolen cars— without actually apprehending a suspect—as *another crime solved by the FBI*.

The hypocrisy and inefficiency drove my dad crazy— What about catching criminals? he kept protesting. After ten months he was completely disillusioned with the FBI. Two incidents amplified his frustration. He found out that there were agents in each of the fifty-two field offices across the United States whose only job was to sit around and watch TV, listen to the radio and read the newspapers looking for any mention of Hoover, which was then immediately reported to Hoover's loyal lieutenants, who investigated the perpetrators. This discovery coincided with the firing of Agent Carter. Carter was caught alone with a girl, which was against FBI policy—regardless of the fact that the girl in question was Carter's fiancée. Then two of Carter's colleagues were fired for failing to report Carter's improper relations with his fiancée. Dad concluded that fighting crime was not as important to Hoover as imposing his personal views on the agents that worked for him, so he resigned.

Mom said he was so disappointed by the way Hoover ran the FBI that he didn't care what would happen to him if he wrote the book. It was before Watergate, she said. Most people didn't believe that Hoover could be bad. After *Inside the FBI* was published they tapped our phones, printed false newspaper articles about your dad, basically tried to ruin his reputation, said Mom. The book came out the year you were born. It was pretty scary, wondering if Norm was going to get arrested on some made-up charge, or put in jail for being a Communist or something. He was harassed not only by Hoover himself but by a famous TV personality named Joe Pine, who invited Dad onto his nationally acclaimed show. During the show Joe Pine accused my dad of being a KGB agent, and brought an alleged KGB double agent onto the stage. The agent, big and burly, confronted my dad, which nearly ended in a brawl between them outside the studio. Mom said that Hoover was completely stunned by my dad's audacity—how could this nobody challenge Hoover's integrity when even the president of the United States and Congress wouldn't dare? So Hoover hit him hard.

I studied my dad driving the truck. I thought about his notorious FBI informant Murph the Surf, who used to meet my dad out in the warm Miami surf to exchange information, and years later was busted for stealing the Star of India sapphire. Murph introduced Dad to a beautiful girl that he really fell for. But she was the daughter of a high-ranking mafioso, and when the FBI found out that Dad was sleeping with her, and not *just doing surveillance* like he had claimed, he had to let her go.

Dad's fingers tapped the steering wheel. I imagined him hanging out with ruthless criminals, sleeping with a mafioso's daughter, then defying Hoover and enduring the assault that followed—dangerous shit. It seemed odd that nobody on Topanga Beach was all that impressed by it. And I realized that no matter who you were, or what extraordinary accomplishments you made, Topanga Beach was always bigger than you.

All that mattered there was surfing. It was the great equalizer. I think Dad loved the purity and simplicity of that.

Up ahead there were pastel-colored buildings and my dad announced that we were entering the town of San Vicente.

We ate lunch at a restaurant off the highway. He looked sad and I wondered if it was because of Sandra. The porch faced the dirt road where we had parked the truck. We ate under a trellis and during the entire lunch my dad's face was sliced in two by the shadow of one of the overhead slats. One of his eyes was lit and the other was dark. It was the first time that he ever seemed guarded, secretive to me. There was no way to know what he was thinking or feeling. I wondered if that's what had bothered my mom so much.

Let's go, I said, wanting to get him into the full light of day again.

The blacktop quivered in the heat and the world was dead and dried out all around us. We drank mineral water and ate peanuts and tossed the shells out the window. Our only jubilant moments came when we had a farting contest. My dad won. Later we squatted and shit in the sagebrush and my dad told me to watch out for rattlesnakes, and then I couldn't go and I was doubled over with a stomachache until we stopped at some town by the water and I used a restaurant bathroom.

After relieving myself I found my dad on the beach playing guitar and singing *Heart of Gold* to three Mexican girls. They were dressed for winter, I thought, and one of them walked right into the ocean with all her clothes on and took a swim. They did that in Vallarta too and I wondered why they didn't wear bathing suits.

A couple of mean-looking guys came out of the bar and stared at my dad and the girls. My dad played on like they weren't there staring at him. One of the guys with a sunburn over his brown skin called out to my dad in Spanish and I recognized the word *gringo* and my dad glanced over at him, his eye bone hooking around and setting his eyeball deep in the socket.

The guy scoffed at my dad. My fingers tingled and I was anxious. The sunburned guy approached my dad and my throat closed. My dad said something to him in Spanish and it took the man by surprise. He didn't speak for a moment and then he said something back. My dad smiled and began playing a Mexican song and sang in Spanish, and some more people came out of the bar and the sunburned guy gestured toward my dad as if he had arranged this little concert with his old gringo buddy.

I walked over and sat next to my dad. Between songs I told him I wanted to go. After my second request he glanced at the ocean.

Yeah. No waves around here. Gotta review the map, he said.

We checked into a cinder block motel and my dad paid the elderly clerk to watch the truck. We parked it in front of our room and kept the yellow curtain open. My dad looked over the map. The red circles indicated a good surf spot he had heard about.

Apparently we'll pass a few tomorrow, he said.

The road cut through shades of gray and as the dawn gave way the dirt turned more golden. Cacti posed like stoic cowboys with the sun still behind the sharp ridges. Nothing but cactus and bush could live out here. It was going to be hot and dusty in a couple of hours and we would spend another day baking in the truck, sticking to the seat, hoping for the air coming through the window to be cool but tasting the dust and slumping there like zombies. I daydreamed about snow, cool and fresh on my face, turning to water on my tongue. I would have given anything to turn back the clock to winter.

Just eight months ago my dad and I had ridden the single-chair chairlift up the face of Mount Waterman. It took an hour and a half to drive his little white Porsche there from Topanga Beach. It was snowing and my dad didn't stop to put on chains because he wanted us to get the first chair and find untracked powder.

The lifty put a blanket over me as I sat on the wet seat and I glided up the slope into the driving snow. I was warm beneath my parka but my face was frozen. I thought about my friend Bobby Citron's birthday party and eating chocolate cake and I hoped I wouldn't miss the party.

At the top we hiked into a cluster of spruce trees that protected us from the wind. My dad's thighs flexed like a racehorse as he sidestepped above me. We reached a nearly square boulder the size of an outhouse and my dad hiked up next to it and looked over the lip of the ridge.

Looks fantastic, Boy Ollestad.

Is it steep?

Just right for all this snow, he said, and I knew that meant it was steep.

I hate it when it's too steep.

I'm going to cut across the ridge and check for avalanches.

Don't fall in.

I won't.

He cut across the ridge and a chunk of snow sloughed off and drained into the gully that dropped from the ridge. A hundred feet below, the gully disappeared in the clouds crawling upward.

Looks good. Go for it, Ollestad, he said from up on the side-wall of the gully.

I kicked and bucked my skis to turn them the right way. I looked down and it was really steep.

The deep snow will hold you up. Don't be afraid to get some speed going, he said.

I dug my poles in and they sunk all the way to the handles. I jerked them out and rocked back and forth until my ski tips broke through, then I began to track downward.

Up and down. Pump your legs, yelled my dad.

I tried to move up and down. The snow was thick and deep, shoveling up against my chest. I wrenched my body in an attempt to turn. Through the snow covering my goggles I saw the side of the gully curving up in front of me. I tried to pump my legs again. Suddenly I pitched forward, releasing from the heel of my bindings, and vaulted head first into the gully wall. Snow plugged my mouth and I couldn't breathe. I strained to move my arms. They were swaddled to my sides. I coughed out the snow, yet every exhale produced an involuntarily inhale. The more I fought to breathe the more snow stuffed down my throat. My mouth would not close.

Boot-first my dad pulled me out. I regurgitated snow. I cried. I yelled every swear word that I had learned on Topanga Beach. He cleaned my goggles and told me he was right there. There was no way I was going to suffocate because he was right there.

When my mountain fit ran out of steam he strapped the goggles back around my helmet and fitted my boots into the bindings.

We should just hike back up, Dad, I said.

It's too deep.

That's why we shouldn't have come here. It's too deep.

It's never *too* deep, Ollestad.

Yes it is. It's too deep to even see or move.

You have to pump your legs right away before the skis submarine.

It's impossible, I said. Why do you make me do this?

Because it's beautiful when it all comes together.

I don't think it's ever beautiful.

One day.

Never.

We'll see, he said. *Vamanos*.

I'm just going to crash again. And it's going to be your fault.

Keep the legs pumping.

I can't.

Then I pushed off and lifted my arms up and out like a bird opening its wings. I meant to prove that I was stuck but my skis rode to the surface.

That's it, Ollestad. Pull the knees up.

Above the gluey snow it was easier to bank my skis. As I sank again I lifted my knees up into my stomach. The counterweight elevated my tips like a ship heaving over a swell and I rocked up and over the next billow of snow. I kept it going, the up-and-down rhythm, wrenching free of the heavy snow before my tips buried. I heard my dad hoot and then a wave of snow splattered across my goggles and I was blind. I swiped at the goggles clearing the left side enough to see another wave hit me, and I swiped again and remembered I needed to pull my knees up. It was too late. I ejected out of my bindings, somersaulted and landed on my back.

I brushed the snow off my face and was able to breathe. I lay there until I heard my dad hooting and I sat up. A wedge of snow rippled toward me down the center of the gully as if an orca tunneled beneath pushing a white wave.

My dad's head appeared for an instant, popping out the top of the white wave. Then he stopped just above me. His mustache was a frozen white sausage. His beige sheepskin jacket and black pants sprouted cotton balls of snow. I caught sight of one of his eyes, electric blue through the rose-tinted goggles, half-crazed like something wild that had just killed and eaten its prey.

Beautiful Ollestad, he said in smoke puffs.

Inside I was jumping for joy but I was careful not to let him see because that would only encourage him and then he'd ask for more.

Can we go home now? I said.

He groaned. You're a real *pulver hund*, he said, and I knew that was German for powder hound.

Wait till you ski Alta, Utah, he said. The powder there's like floating on a cloud.

I caught myself dreaming about superlight Alta powder for a second, then turned away to hide any glimmer from him. Sometimes I detested his charisma, the way it trampled everything and always won out. Yet even then I wanted to be like him.

It was a lot of work to make it to the road in the heavy snow. We hitched a ride from a Cal Trans truck back to the parking lot. I could tell that Dad wanted to ski another run. I even knew the logic of it: *These days are rare and you gotta get 'em while you can.* I wanted to share in his excitement for this golden moment. But I wanted to play with my friends more.

For some reason he didn't push it further that day, and an hour and a half later we pulled up in front of Bobby's house. I ran inside with my ski clothes still on and discovered that the kids had just finished the chocolate cake. I cried and wouldn't talk to or look at my dad. The mothers eyed us—we were out of place in our wet ski clothes and soiled matted hair, and we smelled like sweat. They had come from showers and smelled

like lilacs and we had just crawled out of the woods. Oblivious
to it all my dad charmed the ladies and then scarfed down the
vegetable plate. Feeling rough and dirty compared to everyone
else I stayed in the background, hoping for, but never finding,
a thread of conversation to grab that would tow me into the
gang's banter. I had nothing in common with these kids, and
once again, I yearned to live the life of my peers—riding bikes
together after school, playing ball in a cul-de-sac.

Am I going to miss any birthday parties? I asked my dad as he
cracked open a bottle of water and handed it to me, the Baja heat
coming on early this morning.

None that I know of.

I gave him a bitter look and he added, There will always be
more birthday parties.

I turned away from him, sulking. He patted my back.

You got it easy, Ollestad, he said. Grandma used to drag me
off the baseball field right in the middle of games and make me
go to dance lessons. Imagine that. Shit, all you have to do is go
surfing and skiing, fun stuff.

Shocked, I swung around to face him. Dance lessons? Like
tap-dancing? I said.

Worse. Ballet.

Oh man, I said. Why?

She had a dream, he said, stretching out the word *dream*, of
me being in movies.

In *Cheaper by the Dozen* Dad played the oldest son, twelve or
thirteen years old, and I remembered that in his first scene he
was wearing a baseball uniform.

Was it your idea to wear the baseball uniform in *Cheaper by
the Dozen*? I said.

A smile lifted his whole face.

Absolutely, he said.

That's pretty cool, Dad, I said.

Well, he said, riding that bus for hours to one of the studios and then having to wait like cattle for two or three more hours wasn't cool. I missed a lot of fun for Grandma's dream.

Dad looked like a little boy asking for sympathy, and I knew he was still pissed at Grandma.

Waiting in those lines I'd sleep leaning against the wall, he said.

Didn't you fall down? I said.

He glanced at the road and shook his head.

You made money though, I said trying to make him feel better.

True. That helped me get through college, he said.

We stopped to get gas and eat and then we were on the road again. The road climbed through higher country. The remainder of the day was just a blur of heat, and I nodded off and drank water and stared out the window at the same thing over and over—dirt and chaparral and cactus. I complained about drinking only water. I needed something else, some kind of juice. He gave me a hooked-eyebrow glance and took a showy swig of the water.

Mmm, he said, smacking his lips. Water-juice. It's fantastic.

He handed me the bottle.

Water-juice? I protested.

Try it, he said, as if this were a brilliant idea worth celebrating.

I took a sip.

Mmm water-juice, I said.

. . .

At around sunset the road wound back down to the sea and we spent the night in a hotel near crashing waves. The heat kept me stirring all night and I tried to pretend I was in the cold so that I could sleep. I kept thinking about the trip we took to Alta, Utah, during Easter break.

My dad was brushing his teeth in front of the bathroom mirror at the Little America Hotel in Salt Lake City. I saw his dick hanging in the mirror. His ass was whiter than his legs and the muscles up his spine made a deep groove to his shoulders.

The shower shut off and Sandra stepped out in a waft of mist. Like a ghost I saw her reach for a towel and wrap it around her chest. It hung over her sex and her legs looked really skinny— chicken legs, my dad would tease. She moved out of the mist and saw me watching from the bed and the skin around her eyes twisted. I wondered if she knew that I had watched her straddle my dad last night, across the room on the other bed, her face cringing with pain but her sighs full of joy.

Norm, she said, addressing my dad. Can't you put some clothes on?

You're one to talk, he said with a smile.

It's like a barn around here, she said.

My dad laughed and Sandra closed the toilet room door behind her. My dad walked to the window and slid the curtain all the way open.

There's at least a foot of snow on top of the Porsche, he said.

A blast of wind peppered the glass and he turned his head and shot me a look full of hunger.

Sandra emerged from the toilet wearing long johns. When she saw the blizzard outside she stopped.

You must be kidding me, she said.

My dad crossed the room and his eyes were glazed, lost in some powder-feast. He collected my ski clothes and brought them to me.

Let's go, Boy Wonder.

What's the rush, Norm? said Sandra. Look at it.

Exactly. Look at it. It's a dream come true.

As we rode up the first chairlift and snow pecked at my face I wondered how come Sandra got to sit in the Alta Lodge and sip cognac.

At the top of the lift Dad and I tucked and skated to fight through the driving wind.

Stay in my tracks to the next chair, he said.

The second chairlift was also empty and the lifty hardly acknowledged us. Blown by the wind, our chair clanged against the first tower. Lightning flashed and cut open the clouds and I huddled next to my dad. He nestled his armpit around the back of my neck.

They're going to shut it down, he said. We're lucky we made it on the chair.

Lucky?

Thunder clapped and he didn't respond and I wasn't going to twist from under his wing to see his face.

We slid off the chair at the top of the mountain. I waited with my back against the wind while my dad scouted out the area. He hiked up the ski patrol trail to a ridge.

He looked like a bare spruce tree leaning over the far side of the ridge and I waited for his signal. I heard a whistle. It could be the wind. Then I saw an arm wave.

I hiked up to him. When I looked over the ridge a gust swept dry powder off the long white humps of snow like a swarm of diamonds. A silver cloud tumbled out of the sky and unraveled into tendrils like a ballroom of dancing ghosts.

I can't see shit, I said.

We got to find the trees.

Where are they?

Down there somewhere.

I'm cold.

He rubbed his gloved hand up and down my back.

Go for it, Boy Wonder. Test the snow.

I think we should go back down the regular run, I said.

He shook his head.

As I dropped over the ridge a rising tide of snow reached over my knees and my thighs plowed the sea of white crystals. They blew off my chest and glimmered in a halo around me. The crystals and I moved as one. The clouds and the wind sheared off and nothing seemed to exist outside my crystal ball. I lifted my knees and popped into the air. I came down and the crystals spread away beneath my skis. I steered and there was no resistance, no fluctuation, just one fluid stream of powder. This is what he dreamed about and made him so excited, this powdery nothingness.

I banked like a seagull riding a current of wind and there was nothing more to life than this blind freefall.

I heard my dad yell and felt him glide in beside me—now we were inside one big halo. His sheepskin jacket was all I saw.

Whoosh. The halo shrank and he was gone, shooting down the slope. I was alone again in the weightless cascade.

Trees stood in a row. They reflected light onto the snow under the limbs. No tracks anywhere. Deeper in the woods the snowflakes fell straight down because the forest kept the wind out. I held my turn until I saw an opening where I could enter the woods. I banked and sailed through. The halo sucked away behind me. It was brighter and the snow piled up around the tree trunks and I weaved around them as though they were race poles. The trunk pillows burst apart and the feathers wisped my face. I loved the feeling and I hunted down the biggest pillows I could find. I wanted to show my dad.

Then everything dropped out beneath me. I flipped over. I was upside down. But not falling anymore. Snow poured into my parka from the waist and out the neck and into my hair. When it stopped I saw a tree trunk not more than two feet from my face. Looking downward I saw frozen earth and roots. Upward I saw my skis parallel with the tree's limbs above them. My ski tips were wedged against the tree trunk on a lip of bark. My tails rested on the outer rim of the tree well in which I hung upside-down.

I reached upward for my skis. The bark cracked. Too fragile. I pinned my chin to my chest and yelled.

Dad. Dad!

It was quiet. What if my dad can't find me? He'll have to go down and back around. But he might think I've quit already and go to the lodge. Snow will cover my tracks if he doesn't come soon. He'll never find me. I'll freeze to death.

Dad! Dad!

My feet were cold and the blood drained into my head and it got heavy. I unzipped my pants and pulled out my dick. With my teeth I pulled off one glove then cupped my hand around my dick. It was warm. Having something to hold, something so entirely mine, settled me down, and I forgot about freezing to death.

I must have put my penis back inside my pants because when I felt a tug on my ski I was not holding it anymore.

Boy Ollestad! said my dad.

Tears and coughing.

It's okay, he said. I'm here.

He crashed into the tree well and my skis broke from their perch and we both fell onto the frozen ground. My helmet smacked the trunk and one of my skis smacked my dad's shoulder.

You all right? he said.

I guess, I said.

He clicked off my skis. When he stood up his head was just below the top of the well.

I'm going to throw you out, he said.

He grabbed my waist. Hoisted me onto his shoulders. Interlocked his hands in my hands and straightened his arms as I straightened mine.

Put your boots on my shoulders, he said.

I lifted my knees and steadied the boots onto his shoulders. He moved forward and I sprang over the top of the well. I landed facefirst then crawled away from the well.

My skis came flying out next. Then my dad's head appeared. He wedged one boot and one hand against the trunk and the tip of the other boot and the other hand into the snow wall—spread like a starburst. His arm shot up and he grabbed a limb and snow ruptured from the pines and caked his head. He twisted, pushing both boots off the trunk to dive. He landed next to me.

He shook his head like Sunny coming out of the ocean. He lifted his goggles.

That was gnarly, Ollestad.

I know.

How 'bout that powder?

I was looking at the tree well and in that moment the bliss of the powder was difficult to enjoy. Then I noticed him staring at me. His eyes beamed like a golden sun cutting through the snowstorm and the high seeped back in.

He opened his hand and I took it and he pulled me upright.

We'll head down that valley, he said. Could be some good skiing down there, Boy Wonder.

CHAPTER 11

ROSE FROM my dad's cold limp body. Everything appeared to have slowed down. Each snowflake was separate and unique from the other. The plane debris creaked a specific timbre with every gust. The fog swarmed in discrete braids of vapor.

I crouched on all fours like a wolf or some sort of animal that is used to living in these mountains. I swiveled my neck up and down, eyes tracking the geography of the funnel. I could smell the snow and distinguish the wind in another chute from the wind roaring in this chute. As if wearing ski goggles, I was able to delineate the contours in the snow, no longer a shapeless white mass that I would have to touch in order to discern the changes in texture and pitch.

My mind stopped darting from one thought to the next. No longer debated whether or not the punishing storm would finally win, whether or not I would lose my grip on the ice, or if

Sandra was right or wrong about my dad. My mind sealed itself off from everything but the immediate geography.

I turned away from my dad and stared into the blizzard. Far across the chute a white airplane wing, previously camouflaged by the gray fog blending with the white snow, seemed easily distinguishable, as if suddenly my eyes could cut through the flat, milky light. The wing was lodged against the base of a big tree trunk. The snow was flatter there, having gathered behind the trunk.

I moved toward it, one hand then foot at a time, scaling laterally out of the funnel. The wind gathered razors of ice off the tree limbs and lashed my face. Upslope a few feet the wind had chafed away some of the snow and exposed a faint trail. I tracked higher to root it out, sturdy on my four paws as a mountain goat.

My hands found the scant trail ledge before my eyes saw it. I slinked low to eye the trail's shape and trajectory. It traversed the chute, feathering away near the tree where the plane wing pulsed in and out of existence. The edge of the wing was fused into the snow at the base of the tree trunk. It was propped up at an angle. Shelter.

I thought of the airplane's floor rug. I remembered seeing it tangled amongst some twisted metal near Sandra. I needed it. Also maybe there's an ice axe or shovel or at least some gloves somewhere in the wreckage. So I followed my prints back to the impact zone. Slipping was not an option. I was hunting for tools.

I rummaged through the twisted pieces. Nothing to help me, except the rug. The frayed metal scraps would only cut my hands up, and they weren't stiff enough to axe with. I coiled the rug and hefted it under what would be my downhill arm during the hike back to the wing.

I heard Sandra whimpering. She was above me—I had tuned her out along with everything else that was a distraction. Her eyes were glassy, lashes frosted. I told her to carefully, slowly, step-by-tiny-step, move with me to the wing.

No, she said. I can't move.

CHAPTER 12

*D*AD WAS HOLDING both our surfboards when I woke up, and it took a second to remember that we were in Mexico.

Let's get wet, he said. It'll feel good.

I was suspicious because he didn't mention the waves at all, just the part about getting wet. I followed him down some rusty metal stairs and we passed a Mexican couple dressed up in fancy linen clothes. They huddled against the railing as if we were *banditos* or lepers or something. Down on the beach the swells became waves, big waves.

It didn't look so big from up high, I said.

You'll be fine. There are some beautiful peelers coming off that point. See them?

Should I surf the inside section?

Hell no, he said. If you don't surf the point you might as well be anywhere riding the whitewash.

I swallowed any further protests because I could see in his eyes that we were going out no matter what.

Although the air was as hot as a two-dollar pistol, as my dad liked to say, the water was cool. I howled because the salt stung my raspberried hip and the scrapes on my ass and arm and hand.

It's good for it, he said.

I clenched my teeth and put my head down and paddled. The stinging waned and after ducking under a few waves I felt awake and clearheaded for the first time in days. He pushed me through the bigger walls of whitewash and the salt scrubbed off the caked layers of sweat.

Out on the point I shivered, more from buried fear than the water temperature. My dad rubbed my back and spoke softly to me about the waves and how a ride could be effortless, like a seagull gliding an inch off the surface.

The swells came around the headland and stood up without warning. They were taller than my head. He told me I could do it, that it would be *no problemo,* and he turned my board around and told me to paddle for the *little one rolling in.*

He pushed me into the wave. Not a *little one,* it was over my head. I swept my feet under my body and leaned back just a bit. The nose of the board dove for an instant and then planed out on the bottom. I turned my shoulder and the board responded perfectly, elevating into the face of the wave. I pumped my back leg to generate speed.

My dad said these waves were perfect because they broke down the line without sections. I hoped he was right because no matter how hard I gyrated I remained in the crux of the wave— right where the face of the wave bent and the lip of the wave started to pitch outward. I kept pumping my legs and the lip kept pitching toward my head. After a string of near escapes, each one a victory, my legs got tired and I curved over the lip and down the back of the wave. I paddled to the beach before my dad could call me back out.

The sand was black and burning hot so I sat on my board. I watched Dad ride some waves. He swung his board up the face of the wave, banking off the pitching lip, which drove him down the face, giving him enough speed to thrust off the bottom and back up the face to bash the lip again.

We ate lunch in a restaurant at the top of the rusty stairs. We sat at a pigskin table in our wet shorts and the refined Mexican couple scrutinized our sandy feet and salt-contorted hair. My dad sunk low over the table and shifted his eyes to the couple and back to me.

They have no idea what they're missing, he said.

His eyes wound up. His cheeks formed into two rosy balls.

They think they're really something, he said. We just surfed perfect waves, perfect, with nobody out, and they're just sitting there oblivious, sipping coffee and chatting about who knows what.

I looked over at the fancy couple. They sipped their coffee like birds and the man smoothed out his linen shirt and I thought about us racing across the sea on those waves.

It would be boring to be them, I said.

Could you imagine? he said, and we laughed like two monkeys.

In the morning a crosswind was chewing the swells down to one-foot mushers. We left and never found another good wave in Baja. After traversing the monotonous desert all morning we parked on a bluff of dust and sand, no bushes or plants or color, except for the emerald sea below. Just looking at it cooled me down.

Good thing we got those waves yesterday, he said.

It's sure better than sitting in a hot truck all day with nothing to look at but dust, I said.

He laughed.

Have you ever been tubed? he said.

No.

It's kinda like flying through deep powder.

Really?

Yeah. Even though it's different, you get that *feeling*.

I turned and my dad was staring at me with wild sapphire blue eyes. He saw it in me and I saw it in him—a remembrance of that feeling: hovering in a weightless space with honey on the tip of your tongue and pure red blood gorging your heart, soaring on a current of angelic music cutting clear mountain air.

Maybe we'll find some tubes for you, Boy.

What happens if you don't make it out?

You get crushed.

He punctuated his response by holding his gaze on me.

My dad was not his usual self that night. We ate in a town crowded with Mexican tourists and he scowled and stared at the people moving along the cobblestone street. It seemed like he was glaring at women's asses a lot. He said he was feeling under the weather and he ate oranges and raw garlic with cheese for his dinner.

Are you sad about Sandra?

Naw. I'm just fighting off a bug.

Will she be there when we get back?

I don't know. I hope so.

In the room we plugged in the fan he had bought at the local hardware store. The store had mostly barren shelves and

was dank and dirty, part of a broken world of half-built structures and unfinished roads. We sat naked on our respective
beds receiving alternate blasts from the fan. He tuned the guitar, which was way out of tune from the heat. He sang *Blue
Eyes Crying in the Rain* and then shut off the lights.

The following afternoon we set across the Sea of Cortez aboard
the ferry. The only thing good about the eighteen-hour journey would be the cool air coming off the water. My dad played
poker with a Scandinavian doctor and his beautiful wife. There
were stacks of 1,000 and 10,000-note pesos building up in front
of my dad's seat. I wondered if he was trying to impress the
wife. She had dove-white hair and lime green eyes. The opposite
of Sandra.

The dolphins rode waves off the ferry's bow as the sun went
down. I was mesmerized. They must be the best surfers in the
world.

In the middle of the night I was awakened. My dad was curling up on the end of our bench, putting the top of his head close
to mine. He smelled funny.

What's that smell? I said.

We've been sweating for a couple days, he said.

You smell like that lady, I said.

We danced together after you went to sleep, he said. Her
perfume must've got on me.

Where was her husband?

He danced too.

Yeah sure, I thought.

.   .   .

The next morning we disembarked in Mazatlán and the sage was gone, replaced by jungle. The jungle crawled across the hills and was deep green and smelled of wet earth. *This* is Mexico, I thought.

We took the highway south and drove out to the first point we came to. A blond surfer, clearly an American, was waxing up his board.

Guard the truck, said my dad and jogged across the beach and spoke to him.

When my dad returned he looked excited.

The guy thinks the waves will get good today from a hurricane off the coast. What do you say we drive for a couple hours and then surf?

Is it going to get big?

Maybe. But we'll surf a point. Just stay on the inside.

At the last point break there was no inside section where I could ride the smaller waves. I brought this to my dad's attention.

That was unique, he said.

He patted my leg and shut my door and went around to the driver's side.

The road veered inland and I anticipated it veering back toward the coast. I moved to the edge of the seat, waiting for the moment when we'd see the big waves, not wanting them to catch me by surprise. My dad whistled a tune I had heard him play on his guitar and he told me it was Merle Haggard. He jiggled his shoulders and lifted his voice. It was out of sync with the forlorn lyrics and it seemed like maybe he was trying to hide sadness. Or maybe he was fine. There was no way to read him. He was walled off in his own world. I hated not knowing what he was feeling, not having a barometer to look to. Unable to express my aloneness, I felt tied up, and I sat there picking the scab on my elbow.

My dad reached across my body and braked hard, his skin peeling off the vinyl as I banged against the passenger's door. Next to a roadblock made of sandbags and a two-by-four stood a young man in a military uniform that was several sizes too big for him. He waved a white flag.

Shit, said my dad.

What?

Nothing. It's cool. *Federales.*

My dad eased the truck up to the two-by-four that was about hood high. I wanted him to stop farther back. From under a makeshift lean-to of palms appeared three more young men in uniform. The soldiers had rifles over their shoulders, barrels pointed forward and swinging, as they approached us.

Hola, said my dad. *Que paso?*

The teenager with the flag stepped aside and a guy wearing a billed cap took the lead. He was a teenager too. His eyes were small and swollen like Nick's on a Saturday morning. He didn't respond to my dad. The other two guys with rifles circled the truck and glared at me. How could teenagers have guns already? I thought.

I peeked around my dad's body. The leader rested his hand on the nose of the rifle, which was lazily pointed toward my dad's head.

Pasaporte, he said.

My dad reached for the glove compartment and the teenager on my side raised his rifle. The barrel was inches from my face. My dad spoke to the leader in Spanish and pointed to the glove compartment. The barrel dropped and I peed in my pants. I held my breath so I wouldn't cry. I didn't move and the piss ran down my leg.

The leader asked my dad about the washing machine. My dad showed him the Sears receipt. My dad and the leader seemed to argue.

The leader grabbed the door handle and I gasped. The teenagers laughed at me. The leader opened the driver's door and looked behind the bench seat. He yelled to the guy on my side, who opened my door and rummaged through the glove compartment, scattering papers onto the floor and the road. One of them grabbed my dad's guitar. The guy holding the flag made kissing gestures to me. My dad put his hand over my hand and I stared at the black floor mat and the papers.

The soldiers took money from my dad's pockets, then one of them threw the guitar case into the truck bed and a sound rose from my dad's gut. The leader yelled to the kid with the flag and he pulled back the two-by-four. It slid off the sandbags and when there was enough space my dad hit the gas hard. The teenagers whistled and called out.

My dad did not speak. His arm muscles were taut from gripping the steering wheel. I spoke and it startled him.

What? he snapped.

Nothing, I said.

About ten minutes later he pulled over. He told me to change my shorts and I was amazed he had noticed. He fixed the tarp and inspected his guitar. His face looked angry. The vertical crease between his eyebrows cut deep into his skin and it looked like he had a scar there.

Was that all our money?

Almost, he said, then pulled the poker winnings from the sound hole of the guitar.

Ha! I said.

You hung tough, he said.

He kissed me on the cheek.

I love you, he said.

I love you too, I said.

Later that day we came upon another checkpoint. This time I saw only one teenager. He was in uniform like the others had been. He was tall with very dark skin and pimples. He rested something against the sandbags in the shade, and his long spine hooked like the handle of a cane. Gangly legged, he strolled to the truck. He spoke in slow Spanish. He pointed to the washing machine. My dad grumbled and pulled the receipt out of the glove compartment again. On cue the teenager said tax in perfect English. My dad pointed back from where we had come and seemed to recount the heavy tax we had already paid. The teenager looked startled. He craned his head and peered beyond the road into the jungle. Sitting in a folding chair was an older man in uniform with a toothpick in his mouth and a magazine in his hands. The boy whistled and the man tore his eyes from the magazine and shrugged his shoulders, as if bothered. The boy waved the man over.

My dad's eyes darted around. They landed on the sandbags. Suddenly he hit the gas. The tires squealed, then bit, and the truck lurched and charged the barricade. I ducked and heard the wood ping off the grill.

Stay down! he yelled.

He tucked his head between his shoulders like a pigeon and kept the pedal to the floor. I heard a loud pop.

Stay down!

I crouched into the leg space under the glove compartment. I felt the truck pull as we rounded a turn. The truck righted and he looked back.

We're clear, he said.

Holy shit Dad!

I wasn't going to play that game again, he said.

What was that noise?

A gunshot.

Crouched under the dash I stared at his knee thinking about a bullet puncturing his skull.

They don't have a car, I said. Right?

No. They probably get picked up and dropped off.

What about a radio?

Maybe. But probably not.

What if they do?

I didn't see one. I think we're lookin' good.

I crept onto the bench seat and panted like a dog.

Ollestad. Take it easy. We're fine. They're long gone.

I looked at him and he saw the fear and disappointment in my eyes.

I didn't think he'd get to his rifle so fast, he said. He seemed slow.

That was stupid, I said.

He nodded and ran his hand through his curly brown hair. He stared out the window and his eyes were lost in the beaten blacktop. He looked regretful, sort of confused.

I hated being put in this position—shit-in-my-pants scared. Now something worse was happening. Dad looked scared.

What's going to happen? I said.

Nothing.

What if there's another checkpoint?

I'll just have to pay a bigger tax, he said with a smile.

It's not funny, I said.

It was tense for a second there, he said. But we're lookin' golden now.

I kept imagining the bullet tearing open the back of his head. I kept thinking about the checkpoint guards tracking us down and torturing us. The more relaxed my dad became the faster bad scenarios flooded my mind.

I'm never going anywhere with you again, I said.

Ah come on, Ollestad.

I shook my head and we both stared out the windshield. That's how it was for a long time.

I heard thunder crawl over the mountains and soon afterward it started to rain. The road began to descend. I glimpsed the metallic ocean over the tops of the green maze. The view was eclipsed by a canopy of overhanging branches with leaves so thin they looked like paper cutouts veiling the sky beyond.

We hit the coast a few minutes later and pink veins of electricity zapped on and off like neon lights gouging the ocean. I couldn't see the immediate coastline through the jungle, just intermittent swells of ocean out by the horizon.

Silver-dollar raindrops splattered the windshield, drumming the roof, and the swollen ravines on the sides of the road occupied my attention. Suddenly, the truck was skating across the road. My dad braked and the truck tailed out, then the wheels bit and the truck tipped like it was going to roll over. Dad corrected the steering wheel and we waggled back to our side of the road. He glanced at me and smiled like it was nothing.

Curtains of rain moved like giant spider legs across the oily blacktop, trampling into the jungle. The tarp clung to the washing machine. My dad clung to the steering wheel, his knuckles turning white. I mulled over all the bad things I had done in my life. The lies. I wished I hadn't done anything bad because it seemed like that would help us now. I promised not to tell any more lies if we managed to get out of this.

The windshield wipers stopped. My dad wiggled the lever but nothing happened.

Motherfucker, he said.

The windshield immediately gauzed over as if the glass had melted into globs. My dad checked the rearview mirror and rolled down the window and stuck his head out. He pulled over and engaged the emergency brake. He studied his watch.

We have to get off the road.

Where're we going to go?

We'll find a place. *No problemo.*

He took off his shirt and stuck his head out the window and we rolled along the side of the road. Wet hairs draped his forehead and he looked like he was drowning. After a mile he ducked back inside and rolled up the window. With his shirt off I could see his muscles and that made me feel slightly better.

Are we going to drive like this all day?

No.

Why not?

Too dangerous to drive like this, he said.

He checked the rearview mirror and I imagined the older man and the teenager huddled on the side of the road in the rain and an army truck pulling over to collect them.

My dad rolled down the window and stuck his head out again. He looked tough against the rain whipping his face. I knew we had to get off the road because maybe the army guys would catch up with us, but I did not mention it to my dad.

I used all my energy to push that image out of my head and decided to help my dad. It may have been my first truly mature act, knowing that helping him drive through the rain, instead of being stuck in fear, would make me feel better in the long run.

I wiped my hand over the fogged passenger's window and right away I saw a dirt road cutting through the jungle and I yelled to him. He stopped the truck. He backed up. He smiled when he saw the road.

Way to go, Eagle-eye Ollestad. See. Never give up.

He swung the truck out wide and we dropped off the pavement and he told me to hold on. He hit the gas and we tore through the tight opening. The truck bucked and metal grinded and the undercarriage thumped the ground. We waggled our way like a water snake through the deep mud. The trail curved suddenly and my dad yanked the wheel and the ass end of the truck slapped some trees. It went on and on and he couldn't slow down or we'd sink. My eyes were pinned open and I held onto the dashboard and my dad's triceps flexed with every turn of the wheel. His head was out the window flogging like a cowboy on a bull, ducking under jungle limbs and receding within the window frame whenever his side brushed up close to the jungle wall. I almost asked where we were going but decided that would distract him.

Another close call with some part of the truck tagging a branch. My dad hit the gas and we bounced, then sailed for a moment and landed hard, the undercarriage vibrating up through the seat. Then the engine died. The truck halted and we lurched forward. I felt the truck sink.

My dad spanked the steering wheel with his hand and turned to me.

End of the line, Boy Ollestad.

Is the car broken?

I don't know.

Will they find us?

No way José. They'll whip right past that road. We almost did and we were going a quarter of the speed.

I nodded. He seemed right. And he had shared the previously unspeakable-crazy-scary thing with me—that the army guys might come looking for us—and I was comforted by his admission. It's good to be one of the fighters for a change, I thought.

What do we do now? I said.

Walk down to the beach. See if we can find some shelter.

Are there houses around here?

You don't bust your ass cutting a trail like this for nothing, Ollestad.

He carried a surfboard under each arm with his duffle over one shoulder. I carried my suitcase. The mud came up to my knees in some places and we hugged the edge of the trail, searching for firmer ground near the trees. A swath of banana plants gave us something to wedge our feet against and seeing the familiar green fruits clustered around the thick vines reminded me of the plants surrounding Grandpa and Grandma's house.

With each step we had to unplug our feet from the earth. It reminded me of all those hikes I did with my dad in search of virgin powder. I told him so.

Remember your killer snowplow? he said.

Yeah. I could ski anything with it.

You skied the top of St. Anton all the way to the bottom in a blinding snowstorm with ice under the powder in that snowplow.

When did I start skiing parallel?

Let's see. I think in '73 when we took the train to Taos for Christmas.

Oh yeah, I said, recalling the plastic Indian he bought me, and how I would sometimes look at it and think about my dad dying, declaring that I wanted to die too if he died.

Do you think I might win a race this winter?

Don't worry about winning, Ollestad. Just keep trying. The rest will come.

Do you think I'll be in the Olympics one day?

Sure. Better yet you'll get a scholarship to Harvard or Yale.

What's that?

It's when they invite you to go to their school and play a sport for them.

Dad planning my life so far in advance added pressure, as if the mud and the jungle had grown thicker.

Are we ever going to get there? I whined.

My dad stopped. The spackles of mud on his face and mustache and up his legs made him look like some kind of human chameleon of the jungle.

It's easier if you . . .

Just hike straight through without stopping. I know.

He laughed.

Besides there's nowhere to sit down, he said and laughed again.

Not having a place to sit because we were surrounded by mud and jungle and overhead by thick clouds about to burst did not seem even kinda funny.

I wish I didn't come, I said.

And I slogged past him.

Well, Ollestad. I'm glad you did.

I don't want to ski race anymore, I called back without turning. I'd rather do karate.

Your mother's the one who needs to learn karate.

I paused, startled. My dad had never said so much about my mom and Nick before. This was my big chance to speak out—

tell Dad how Nick called me a liar and insisted I'd grow up to be a failure. This was a good time to ask my dad to do something about Nick's cruelty. But all I did was grunt and plod on.

The hillside climbed to a ridge that wandered back toward even bigger hills. Up ahead I saw the trail drop abruptly. Where it appeared again down below, the jungle grew in ribbons over grassy marshland. There were some cows and tall coconut trees and then another hill and I hoped that on the other side finally awaited the beach, shelter and rest.

I guzzled some water. I was sweating and the heat was like a thick cloak and my head burned with a fever.

I'm burning up, Dad.

We'll jump in the ocean and it'll cool you off.

As much as it made sense, that's not what I wanted to hear.

I could feel him looking at me. I wanted him to say something about my mom or Nick. Then I could tell him that Nick swore at me and said I was rotten and said he'd track me down if I told on him. After that, when we got home, Dad would take care of things.

My dad moved behind me and I waited. Then he stopped moving. He didn't say anything.

I threw my suitcase over the drop-off. It appeared a few seconds later floating on the mud in the trail below. My eyes blurred with tears and my voice was raked by anger, *fucking this* and *fucking that*. I sat in the mud and threw globs of it at my dad. Eventually I ran out of steam and just cried. The mud felt good against the scab on my hip. It began to rain again.

Are you done with your mountain fit? he said.

No, I said.

He reached down and I took his hand and he tugged me out of the mud.

Slide down on your ass, he said.

We slid down the hill into the grassy marshland. The mud was waist deep and I grabbed my surfboard from my dad and floated on it.

Great idea, Ollestad.

Where's your bag? I said.

Left it up there, he said. Guess I'll have to wear trunks from now on.

We got to the other side of the marsh and I noticed that some of the mud had dried on our skin—it had stopped raining—and we looked like swamp things. We could hear the ocean and my dad patted my back.

Way to grind it out, he said.

He led me out of the jungle. Abruptly our feet crunched down on a mound of white seashells. I looked ahead and the shells mushroomed all the way to the wet sand and then lay scattered about, washing around on the shore.

The water was blueberry, like the sky now. There were slicks of turquoise where the reef ceased, allowing the white sand to reflect back up through the water. Farther out a bigger reef made swells leap up everywhere like a sea of cobras striking ten at a time. We two swamp things looked on in awe.

For the first and only time my dad refrained from pointing out the beauty. He said nothing. Not even about the surf. He tiptoed over the shells and dove into the ocean. The mud left a stain in his wake. He told me to keep my clothes on in order to clean them out. I opened my eyes underwater and yellow fish scatted beneath a cluster of reef.

We stripped nude and hung our clothes on a papaya tree. The fruit's sweet aroma mingled with the humid air and stuck to the inside of my nose. The yellow-green melons hung like big breasts and I held the papayas' bouquet in my lungs. Everything glared vibrant with color and at the same time was as soft as velvet.

We stood in a daze, our long trudge affecting us now. Time passed and the sweetness of the air and the berry palettes in the sky and water resonated over the percussion of waves crashing against the reef.

Breaking the spell my dad asked me about my hip.

It's getting better, I said.

Sure looks like you got it skateboarding.

I paused. Down here in Mexico, my lie appeared such a small thing.

I did, I said.

Your secret's safe here in Mexico, he said.

My face contorted into a smile. I felt loony and relieved. I charged the ocean and called out, attacking some imaginary demon. The shells sliced into my feet and I dove headlong into the sea.

I surfaced and my dad gave me a humorous sideways glance, then danced over the shells with his balls swinging. He jumped in and floated on his back and watched the sky. He was at ease like a seal bathing with one flipper up and he watched the pregnant thunderheads and seemed to enjoy their warm mist.

I swam ashore and scoured the beach, finding some thick white shells with holes in them. I showed them to Dad and we decided they were puka shells. I collected at least a hundred, storing them in a large abalone shell.

My dad tore open a papaya with his thumbs. We each dug out the slimy black seeds with a shell and spooned the meat into our mouths.

Just like the Indians, he said.

He told me that they fished with handmade spears, carved boats out of logs, and had no TV or cars or restaurants.

They were tough, Ollestad, he said.

How tough?

Tougher than tiger shit.

What's tougher? Tiger shit or tiger piss?

Hmm. Tiger piss maybe.

Really?

Yeah. Probably.

He washed off the surfboards in the salt water and I washed off my suitcase. Then I followed him north.

What happens when you boil to death? I said.

You dehydrate and finally die.

What happens when you freeze to death?

You're cold. Then you feel warm and sleepy. And then you fall asleep and never wake up.

I'd rather freeze to death.

Me too.

We followed the raised sand spit hooking out to sea. My dad looked back toward the big reef. He stopped and studied the waves and I pretended not to notice.

Might get good when the wind settles down, he said.

I didn't respond and he turned and walked around the spit. On the other side was a patch of sand ending where the big black rocks bordered the cove. As we got closer I saw two fishing boats on the wet sand, rocking like cribs. They're not canoes carved from wood, I thought. Little dories overstuffed with nets and buckets and spears—metal not bamboo.

Look, my dad said.

Barely visible above a hedge line of mangroves was a group of steeple-shaped roofs made from coconut palms.

My dad shook his head as if he couldn't believe it and I realized we were lucky. It made me nervous that we were relying on luck.

He followed a path trampled into the shells.

Should we just walk right in? I said.

He opened his hands.

I don't know what else to do, he said.

But what if the people who live here don't like strangers?

Then we'll leave. Don't sweat it, he said.

He took my hand and we walked toward the roofs.

CHAPTER 13

S*ANDRA REFUSED TO MOVE* and the airplane's floor rug was under my arm. Sandra needs an adult to order her under the wing, I thought. Not an eleven-year-old kid that she thinks is a brat. I put the rug down beside her and crawled back toward my dad.

I needed to smell him, feel his skin. There wasn't much I could do without him—I could not move him or Sandra on my own. Why hadn't he woken up? I must be doing something wrong. What the hell is it?

I crossed into the funnel, and navigating the ice curtain drove away all extraneous thought. The fog heaps and wind and snow seemed to erase the terrain and I had to go on my memory of where I thought he was—down a couple feet then across fifteen feet or so. My laser focus held all thought noise at bay. Until I found him.

I nudged my nose into Dad's ear. Cool but not cold. With the crown of my head I rammed him, like an animal might. He was dead weight. I couldn't accept that I was too weak to carry him to the shelter.

You're too heavy, I said, blaming him for my weakness.

My chest thumped with frustration. I put my hands over my face. I turned away from him. I drew my fingers down my face. Finally I opened my eyes. Then clawed up and over to Sandra. I dug into the mountain, cursing it and everything that was mounting up against me—even Nick pointing out my *weak character*, my *inevitable failure*—all the way to her seat. Nick's full of shit, I declared silently as I took Sandra's hand. She shied away from me. I flicked open her seat belt buckle and pulled her out.

Let's go, I said, reminding myself of my dad—how he always took care of her. It was my job now.

What are you doing? she said.

For a moment I recalled her sitting on a bar stool, in Utah maybe, scolding me for being a spoiled brat because I was insisting that my dad leave the boring bar and go down to the game room.

Then I saw that her skin had lost its caramel color, turned pasty from the extreme cold. She's just scared, I decided.

I set the rug behind her seat, hoping it wouldn't get blown away. I moved beneath Sandra and lodged my hands below her fancy leather boots.

Move with me, I said. We're crossing to the wing. We can get under it.

I talked her through it and she followed my instructions. I used my entire body—knees, pelvic bones and chin—to crab us off the edge of the funnel.

My knee caught the corner of the trail first. I guided Sandra's boots onto the ledge and told her she could put pressure on it. Relieved, I rested for a moment.

Great, I said. Now turn onto your side and sort of walk while you lean against the hill.

Sandra's hip and shoulder plowed into the mountain as her boot heels dug into the trail and her good arm helped drag her across the chute. The trail saved us a lot of time and energy. About ten minutes later we slid onto the relatively even ground behind the big trunk.

I have to get the rug, I said.

No. Don't leave.

I'll be right back.

What if you slip?

I grunted and moved upward to find the trail. Millions of specks jumped off the ledge like white fleas, making the ground appear raised. Trudging on I found the rug behind the seat, then paused, wondering about my dad. I wanted to feel him again. I tried to locate him amongst the dizzying gray formations. Streaking white flakes rained down on me and a turbine of wind seemed to shake the mountain.

I have to get warm, I told myself.

I strode away from him on my four paws. I felt my muscles bulging out of my shoulders. My body seemed to have already adapted to what my mind was unwilling to accept—I was on my own.

CHAPTER 14

*D*AD'S CURLY HAIR had dried in a big puff. I stayed right on his tail as he led us toward the coconut palm roofs. I wished he were wearing a shirt or shoes. Not just surf trunks.

The path squeezed between the mangroves and widened to a muddy trail that cut through the tiny village. Except for the mangrove trees abutting the sand, most of the jungle had been cleared away and replaced with caladium and hibiscus and aloe vera plants. The huts looked like old-fashioned schools, made of palms, without windows, except the hut on the end was shaped like a cone and open on the bottom so you could duck under and enter it from any side.

Women and children and old people swarmed around two center huts. They stopped and stared when they saw us.

My dad called to them. No one moved except a little girl who waved to us. She was dressed in a tattered skirt. Most of the mothers wore ragged clothes of all styles and colors. Only the older men looked uniform—thin ponchos, baggy cotton pants and deeply lined faces. Nobody wore shoes. The women's clothes were ornate with gold stripes and ruffled hems like Vegas dancers, the material especially threadbare and faded.

Donde esta los hermanos? Los padres? said my dad.

A woman pointed and rambled quickly in Spanish.

Gracias, said my dad.

We crossed over the mud path along a tree limb that had been laid down, balancing one foot in front of the other like longboarders walking to the nose. The children stared at me as if I were a green-tentacled Martian.

My dad led me around the farthest hut, where chickens scattered from a pile of seeds and took cover behind a pen. Inside were pigs. Big and fat and black. Behind the hut was a grove of widely spaced *tamarindo* trees. The jungle grew thick and heavy right up to the meadow and under the overhang was a stable of horses. Four men worked on four horses, cleaning, shoeing, and feeding them. All the men wore cowboy hats and boots. I had never seen big horses like that in Mexico—just burros. My dad waved to them and they turned and watched us approach, although none stopped their work.

The shortest darkest of the bunch left his horse and met my dad at the gate. He had a mustache like my dad's, but black. He looked about my dad's age, but his oily dark skin made it difficult to be sure.

My dad apologized for his shirtless appearance, and he pointed into the jungle and I recognized the word *auto*. The man called back to one of the cowboys who was wiping down a horse and he nodded without skipping a beat or looking. The man turned back to my dad and gestured toward the huts. My dad thanked him and we left.

What did he say?

We're in luck. They have a place for us to sleep.

I don't want to spend the night here.

We don't have a choice, Ollestad.

I'd rather sleep on the beach.

In the rain?

Maybe it won't rain.

Maybe, he said. What are you afraid of?

I don't know, I said. Can't we just find a hotel or something?

He laughed. We passed the pigpen and came upon the main trail. The kids stared at me again.

It's your hair, said my dad. They probably have never seen blond hair.

Never ever?

Probably not.

Wow.

There were things I had never seen, like Mars or teenagers with guns, and I had never imagined I could be one of those things to somebody else.

We walked across the tree limb and found the path to the beach. I looked back and everyone was still standing there watching us, doing nothing else but watching us.

When we reached the sand he told me to collect my puka shells, and I did. He also gathered more pukas. Then we headed back to the village. He told me to give one of the abalone shells full of pukas to the first girl I saw. It would be a gift for their kindness.

As we came through the barrier of mangroves a young woman stood on the bare back of a horse, across the trail, picking papayas off a huge tree.

Buenas tardes, said my dad.

She teetered for a second then found her balance. She shot him a scornful look, nodded and cut her eyes away. Her hands kept feeling the papayas. She was a real beauty. Black hair, thick and shiny all the way to the middle of her back. Long arms, smooth and brown. Sleepy dark eyes. A slightly curved-down nose. Snarly lips. A scar under her eye. She was not like any girl I had ever seen before.

Give them to her, I heard my dad say.

I snapped my eyes over to him. I shook my head.

Come on, he said. Just set them down.

I was confused. Then I did what he said. We walked away and I glanced back and she was gone.

My dad handed the rest of our pukas to the first grown woman we saw. She was an elder and she sat outside the center hut, watching over things. She said *gracias* and she wasn't opposed to looking into my dad's eyes like the young woman had been. Someone pulled my hair and jolted me out of my stupor. I turned around and a little girl was running away shouting. My dad told me to let them touch it. I stood stiffly and the kids inched up to me as if I were a rabid dog. One of the mothers shooed them away and spoke to my dad while the entire village surrounded us, staring at us. My dad seemed impervious. I watched the ground.

Someone gave my dad two blankets and I followed him to the cone-shaped hut on the end. The entire village moved with us and stood outside the hut even after we entered a slitlike doorway. My dad put the blankets down and laughed. I laughed too. It was strange seeing all those eyes peeking through the slit.

The glamorous life of a rock star, he said.

We sat there trapped for a long time. Then the *vaqueros* arrived and dispersed the crowd. The short guy with the mustache poked his head through the slit. My dad laughed at whatever he said and they suddenly seemed like friends. When the *vaquero* left an elderly woman with no neck brought us beans and tortillas and a drumstick.

Is it from those chickens outside?

Uh-huh.

Do they eat the pigs too?

Yeah. *Carnitas.*

I put the drumstick down, then my dad made me take three bites. By the time he was finished eating it was dark. We set the plates near the doorway and felt our way back to the blankets.

What do we do now?

Sleep.

I insisted on lying close enough to touch him. There were bug noises and a few human-sounding noises and it was so black I could not see the pathway right outside the hut. We were lost in complete darkness and buried away at the edge of a jungle, and Topanga Beach didn't seem so isolated, or even very wild, anymore.

I dreamed of the papaya picker slaughtering a pig before the roosters woke me. My dad was gone. I sat up with a start, confused about where I was. Scattered clouds hung outside the slit. The path was already caking under the bald tropical sun. Sweat made my whole body sticky. I called for my dad. I went to the slit and peeked out. The village was empty. It was eight or nine o'clock, I guessed. A fragment of sunlight burned my cheek and I wondered what it would be like at noon.

I crossed the broken tiles of mud and searched for the path to the beach. The clouds over the ocean cracked in the same

pattern as the dried mud. There was no one around and a rush
of panic made me move too quickly over the shells and they cut
my feet.

My dad was helping lift a net full of fish out of a dory. Two
elders hauled one side and my dad hauled the other with one
hand grabbing the middle. The elders sweated under their ponchos and palm-woven hats, juxtaposing my dad's minimalist
wardrobe of surf trunks.

Take the other side, he said.

I hooked my fingers into the slimy net. A dying roosterfish,
eyes stuck open, looked right at me. We put the net down outside one of the middle huts. Inside the hut I counted five palm-
woven mats edge to edge on the ground. How many people slept
in there?

Let's get wet, said my dad.

My dad was way ahead of me when I stepped out of the hut. A
stampede of kids appeared. I turned my back on them and got
a good grip on my board and walked quickly toward the beach.
The kids trampled over the shells and looked down at me from
both sides of the path. A couple of boys ran their fingers over
the surfboard and fired questions at me.

Surfing, I said, fashioning my hand into a surfboard riding
an imaginary wave in the air.

I saw my dad way out on the sand spit gazing at the surf. The
waves were eclipsed by the slight rise of the spit and his arms
hung blithely at his sides, the board dangling. He was motionless. Big surf, I thought. Shit.

Some of the kids lost interest in me and lagged behind and
the others began throwing rocks and shells into the ocean. I
slowed my pace and hoped my dad would disappear around the

spit. I was barely moving and thought about just sitting down. But if he turned and saw me lollygagging it might piss him off.

The kids spotted a turtle and surrounded it and hucked rocks at it. They poked it with a stick as it shimmied toward the safety of the ocean. I wanted to yell at them but it was their beach and every beach was different with its own rules. So I walked on.

There was a horse tied up near a papaya tree where the jungle met the beach. I wondered which *vaquero* was here. When I came up behind my dad on the sand spit I startled him and he became flustered for a moment. His mouth opened like he was going to say something but closed a second later. He walked off the spit and down the beach.

I stepped into his footprints and peered out. Just offshore I saw her—those snarling lips and the scar under her eye so distinct. She floated on her back and her breasts stood out like big acorns, firm and brown. The smell of papaya fruit was all around and in that instant I named her Papaya. I watched her and my arms hung and I was dead still, a miniature version of the man standing in this place only moments before. Had my dad been watching her? Did she know? Then her eyes opened. They tracked all the way into the corners and only then did she see me.

She flipped over and dove. She swam along the white ocean floor, her brown color beautiful like a trail of brown sugar. She popped up far enough away that I could not see her body through the clear water. She seemed to catch her breath looking out toward the big reef and then she swam farther out.

My dad was way down the beach and I saw his footprints going past her yellow T-shirt and white skirt. I knew that my dad had been watching her but I didn't know if she had let him and only afterward had been surprised by me, or whether she had been surprised that anyone was there at all.

I looked for her and saw her splashing halfway out to the reef. It worried me that she might get tired and drown. I envisioned paddling hard and whisking her out of the deep sea and onto my board. She thanked me. You're safe now, Papaya, I said.

My adrenaline was pumping. Then a gaggle of kids rounded the spit, apparently finished with the turtle and ready to pursue some new curiosity. Full of erratic energy I trotted down the beach.

My dad was waxing his board and mixing sand into the wax when I finally reached him. He studied me and it seemed like we both were starstruck and speechless and floating in some weird space.

Cleaned up nicely, said my dad, glancing at the reef.

Totally, I said.

The Mexican kids must have thought we really were aliens the way we just lingered there—the heat and the aroma and the girl congealing into an orgy of sensations, and Dad and I laughing like drunken half-wits.

I was close to the reef and my dad was behind me for some reason. Coming out of the trance, I realized the waves were twice my size. I sat up on my board. The reef halted the swell's forward momentum and the swell lurched upward then heaved outward, hollowing out the face of the wave. The leading crest was pointed like an arrow as it knifed down and impaled the surface of the ocean. My dad paddled up next to me.

Perfect left-hand tubes. I'll be damned, he said. I'll be goddamned.

A vein rippled with thumping blood from his bicep to his shoulder and his eyebrows forked down over the bridge of his nose, as if he were a savage poised to attack.

I felt ridiculous—these waves were too big and strong for me.

A tube like that will change your life, he said.

I don't want to change my life, I said.

Another swell bared its vicious claw.

You want to watch it for a while? he said.

I thought about it. Yes meant that later I would stop watching and actually try to surf it. No could mean that I wanted to surf it now.

I shrugged.

I'll test it out, he said.

This was a reef wave, a quick combustion of energy that lasted about six seconds, nearly opposite the long reeling point break in Baja. The reef wave dissolved where the water got deep again, where there was an opening in the reef—the channel. My dad paddled through that opening and out past the reef, before cutting over to the take-off spot. In the unlikely event that I would decide to paddle out, I felt that the channel would protect me, and once out there, if a giant set came I could take refuge in its safe harbor.

My dad paddled for the next swell. He got right under the peak and a tumult of water gathered from the floor of the wave and shot up the face, loading the lip. The heavy lip stacked over the face of the wave, separating my dad's board from the coveted arc where a surfer did his thing, and my dad was stuck on the roof. He gripped the rails of his board, sat up and leaned back. Just as the roof collapsed against the reef, the nose of his board ripped free and Dad spun around out to sea. Barely avoiding getting pummeled against the reef.

Faintly I heard voices. I turned and the beach was alive with cheering kids. Behind them the dark jungle flourished as if about to gobble them up. Rounding the sand spit came the *vaqueros* on horseback. One of the boys from the village was in the lead.

I looked for Papaya's yellow shirt against the shells, but it appeared to be gone. The *vaqueros* made their way along the wet sand and the horses shied away from the lapping waves.

The horses stopped in a perfect row and their shadows fell onto the wet sand. The *vaqueros* looked out at us and waited. It struck me that the *vaqueros* had left whatever work they were doing because they expected to see something extraordinary.

Immediately I paddled for the channel. The channel was safe. Deceptive because it appeared to be in the line of fire yet was just out of reach of the wave's angry bite.

As I got closer I heard a groan rising from the reef. Not understanding where the noise was coming from, I sat up. When the next wave came I watched closely. As the swell wrenched and dragged at the reef the groan sounded. At the same time the crest pitched outward, transforming the wave into a tube. I looked into the big oval eye zooming toward me. There was something peaceful about the inside of the tube. Then the eye blinked shut and the wave exploded against the reef.

I glanced to shore. I saw the *vaqueros* astride their horses staring at me and I was sure they understood that I was hiding in the channel and that I was a coward. Then Papaya came around the spit on horseback and the disgrace was unbearable.

To make matters worse my dad waved me into the lineup. I wiped my eyes, pretending to have salt in them. I simply chose not to look up and floated there for a while. Nonetheless every second seemed to double the weight on me. I felt the *vaqueros* watching and Papaya watching and the pressure kept mounting. It finally broke me and I started paddling.

The doubt came right away. It felt like poison under my skin and my head rang. I even imagined Nick laughing at me. He was there helping feed the poison.

I looked up to get my bearing, to make sure I was following the channel out far enough past where the swells hit the reef. Just then a big wave stormed down the reef. The fear it unleashed was like a headwind. I tried to paddle but the headwind beat me back. A burning heat amassed from this friction. I vibrated and coughed and suddenly an ember broke free and seared through me. I stopped paddling.

I searched the clean clear water, trying to gather courage. The hot fear was spreading. I mashed my teeth and imagined a toxic ball beating like a heart inside me. The ball spit its toxic juice through my body, eroding my will. I hated the fear more than anything, so I focused all my hate onto its source, hoping to overpower it.

Fueled by this hatred, my arms oared again. The current wrapping around the reef into the channel shoved me backward. I paddled harder. As I came over a swell I saw my dad dropping into a cavernous pit. His back was to the wave and his board wiggled at the bottom, nearly bucking him, and he leaned so far into the bottom turn that his left hand grazed the water. He was unable to bring his body upright and the mighty forces sucked his board up the face. They drew him to the ceiling. For a split second his body stood tall and it seemed like he could just step right onto the roof and walk down the backside of the wave. Instead the wave pitched him out over the reef. He was horizontal to the ocean, his board chasing him, and he fell out of the sky and belly-flopped. He skidded and the lip struck his torso and the explosion of whitewash obliterated him.

I paddled over the wave just before it got me and stroked hard to make it over the next one. Beyond its crest the ocean lay flat. I caught my breath.

I was numb. In a state of shock. Convinced that my dad was fine but that I could never take that kind of beating. Yet, in that moment, I would have rather died than succumb to my cowardice.

I noticed that the smaller waves missed the outer coral heads and peaked inside. With the drop in size came a drop in heft all around. I paddled for the inside zone, unfazed by the fact that if a set came I would get pummeled.

I shook with adrenaline. Fuck being scared, I muttered.

I monitored the ocean like a big cat waiting to pounce. It wasn't long before a four-footer steamed past the outer reef. I paddled under it and the tail of my board tilted and I was look-ing straight down at the white and purple coral heads. I jumped up and stayed centered, fighting the forward pitch of my body.

Get the back foot down, I told myself.

The floor of the wave dug a trench. I swept down the face to the bottom and pressed on my back foot and the nose of the board scooped out a chunk of water as it ripped from the trench. The twisted veins of water pulling off the bottom sent a shock through my board and nearly bucked me off. I leaned hard into the wave. It towered over me. The lip eclipsed the sun and the face of the wave turned dark blue.

My brain protested. A wall of water is threatening to col-lapse onto you. Bail out.

A voice, some kind of knowing force, told me—it opens up. It wraps around. You will fit inside.

Impossible. A mountain is toppling and you are under it and you need to dive out of harm's way.

No. It bends and you fit inside.

Automatically my knees drew up to my chest and the board climbed into the pocket. My eyes closed as I entered the tube.

The groan rumbled. I opened my eyes. An oval window framed the sand spit. The rock spires. The coconut palms. And the groan sucked away and the spinning cavern was silent. The ominous wall had bent and wrapped me in its peaceful womb. I was buried inside a thing that could maim or kill me, yet was cuddling me now—I was stretched between panic and bliss. Everything essential, everything formerly invisible, burst forth and pulsed through me. I was there, in that elusive space—the dream world of pure happiness.

The window changed shape and—whoosh—I emerged and the world came crashing in, noisy and bright and chaotic.

I saw my dad down the line. A dazzling smile. His eyes beamed with love and I felt like a knight bringing home the golden chalice. I rode out over the back of the wave.

Holy cow, Boy Wonder! What a fantastic tube ride!

I nodded and my lips burned against the salt. And I noticed blood trailing down his rib cage. A big gash on his back.

Are you okay? I said.

I'm fine, Ollestad.

It's bleeding real bad.

It looks worse than it is.

I remembered my mom telling me the same thing about her black eye.

So how was it? he said.

Just . . . I searched for words, images. All that I could grasp was the feeling—I had never felt so good in all my life.

I don't know. Radical, I said.

He held my gaze as if perfectly attuned to the ecstasy spiking and reverberating in every part of me.

You've been to a place that very few people in this world have ever gone, he said. Someplace beyond all the bullshit.

We drifted and thought about the perfect place I had been, and the ocean grew very calm. My dad bled into the water and the threat of sharks was somehow negated by my tube ride, as though we were invincible because we were a part of everything. I looked around and this strange world suddenly made perfect sense.

CHAPTER 15

S ANDRA WAS CURLED up into a ball near the wing and
I was startled when she grabbed my arm, squeezing
viciously.

How can he be dead? she said. How can your dad be dead?

I growled like the wolf that I had imagined I had become
and her question got rejected, spit out, before my brain could
fully absorb it. A layer of rough hide seemed to grow over my
cold skin, shielding the snow and wind and bad thoughts, and I
hunkered and drew it tighter to my body. Then I slithered under
the wing. I lay the rug over the snow and tucked it against the
back edge of our shelter.

Get under the wing, I said.

She crawled under and I crawled in after her. She wrapped
her arms around me. Two animals huddled in their cave.

I hope they come for us, she said.

Go to sleep, I said. Rest.

Are we going to die? she said.

No, I said, then wondered if we would freeze to death waiting here for someone to rescue us.

It got warm under the wing with Sandra wrapped around me and I faded into sleep.

As I dreamed I knew it was the same dream that I had dreamed before I woke up the first time after the crash. I wondered how many hours ago that was. Or was it less than an hour ago? In the dream I float upside down. My blue Vans above my head. A luminous white oval encapsulates me, black beyond its edge. At the top of the oval seeps a granular light. I drift feet first toward the light and ask myself what is happening. Calm and lucid comes the answer: You're dying. Oh, I'm dying, I say back to myself with wonder. Something is pulling me down. I can't quite reach the granular light, the cracked doorway. Two hands, two currents—no, a wave-shaped force pitches over me. Holds me from floating up into the granular light.

He jumped over me, I said, and my voice woke me from the dream.

Sandra was wrapped around me tight. Her hands were very cold. I turned and snuggled her, my face nestled against her neck. I envisioned my dad jumping over me as the plane broke apart. He saved my life and I would find a way to save his. I held this hope in my mind even though some part of me knew it was too late. Melting into Sandra's body I dozed again.

A muffled thwack against the air woke me. It repeated itself and I couldn't understand what it was and it came and went like the waves of fog.

I noticed Sandra's watch. It was still ticking. I thought of the commercial catchphrase *Takes a licking but keeps on ticking*. I looked closely, and it was a Timex. It was nearly twelve noon, the big hand and little hand both near the twelve, and I laughed.

What's happening? she said.

It's still ticking, I said.

What's going to happen to us, Norman? she said.

I did not know what to say. I thought about how long we'd been up here. We took off around seven, I remembered. So it's been five hours. What the hell have we been doing? Then the thwacking noise got closer and I identified it. I slithered from under the wing and rose off my belly onto all fours.

Where are you going? said Sandra.

I hear a helicopter, I said.

The fog was breaking and the sky was patched with black-edged clouds and the strips of blue looked far away. I had to get out from under the broad reach of the spruce limbs. The light was brighter now and the trail was trodden from my two trips back and forth and I scampered across the chute. The thwack of the blades was gone again and I wondered if I had imagined it.

For the first time I could make out the chute's broader features. As I had guessed, it was shaped like a half-pipe carved vertically down the mountainside, dropping for at least twenty yards, maybe more below the receding clouds. The icy chute was bordered by chunks of rock. The rocks hemmed us in and trees grew out of the rocks with snow filling in the nooks and crannies like mortar. A slick, icy groove washed straight down one side of the chute—the funnel. Instinctively I understood that the funnel was the predominant fall line where your skis would gravitate, the most direct and thrilling way down. I wanted nothing to do with it today.

Suddenly rotors boomed overhead again, sending laps of noise against the mountain. I yelled up at the checkered sky. Struts appeared through the shifting pools of smoky fog. I waved with both hands and yelled at the belly right above me. I waved and yelled.

Hey! Right here! Hey!

I thrashed my arms and screamed so loud it burned my throat raw.

Right here! See me?

The helicopter hovered above the treetops. The struts were like the rails of a sled that I could grab.

Just in time, I thought. Dad can't hold on much longer.

I screamed at the 'copter and kept whipping my arms.

Dad. We're saved!

The 'copter dipped to one side and I saw a guy with a helmet and expected him to call back through the loudspeaker. I'll guide them over to my dad and they'll lower down and fly him to a hospital.

My adrenaline spurred me across the chute toward my dad and I motioned to the 'copter to follow. The 'copter powered up. It whined.

I shuffled my feet, careful not to slip, and kept flagging them toward the impact zone. The closer I got to my dad, the funnel, the slower I had to go. Any moment now I'll have to drop to my belly and hug the mountain. I won't be able to flag them. So I stopped where I was. Arms raised high like a ref signaling a touchdown I motioned the 'copter toward my dad. You guys are the greatest. Thank you. Thank you.

Then the 'copter dipped to one side and slowly banked away from me.

Hey! Right here! Wrong way!

A cloud swallowed the blades, then the belly and struts. The thwacking noise thinned. Then faded.

What the hell?

I turned to my dad, who was about fifteen feet away across the chute. Can you believe that?

He was coated with snow like an ice sculpture.

My adrenaline went cold and flushed down my body, leaving me hollow.

I closed my eyes. I pushed everything away. Tough it out. Focus on the next thing. Don't worry about what has already happened.

Did they see you? called Sandra.

No, I said.

She asked more questions, and I was fixed on something way way down below. It was barely visible over the clouds bottled up in the chute. My eyes settled on a flat meadow. The flat spot was unnatural and improbable in this jagged landscape. The round bed of snow glowed woodless and I thought that if I made it there I would be okay. My eyes stuttered, gobbling up the terrain that led to the meadow. How to get there?

Below my feet the chute disappeared under a long blanket of fog. Several hundred feet lower the fog bent with the easing grade and a sparsely wooded slope emerged. As my eyes traced the slope downward the trees gave way to a steep, bald apron of snow. It nosed away so that I could not see how far down it went. The fog made the terrain difficult to follow but I filled in the blanks. As if I were water I flowed with the various gullies and ravines for thousands of feet until the mountain's creases and bulges all seemed to feed into a tight gulch, sandwiched between two walls of glacier-scathed rock. A massive ridgeline grew out of the gulch. It would take hours to climb over it, and it looked too steep, too slick. But the gulch might squeeze through or around the massive ridge. If Dad and I were skiing back here we'd flow right into that gulch and find a way through.

Then I saw a rooftop. It was not far from the meadow. Looking down on it from a couple miles away, I almost did not believe it. My eyeballs strained to segregate the clean smooth man-made shape from the sawtoothed woods. It was definitely a roof.

The woods surrounding the roof were thick except for a furrow that cut toward the meadow. It was some kind of road, a passageway through the dense woods between the roof and the meadow.

I retraced my route down to the meadow. The chute, the wooded section, the long apron of snow curving away into the gulch, the massive ridgeline, then the flat meadow where we could rest before stumbling through the woods to find the shelter chiseled a map in my mind, fixing the meadow as my true north.

I took in the rooftop one more time to make sure. Looks like a ghost-town building, I thought. We can get warm there.

The storm heaved like two waves closing in on each side of me. The respite was over. Bales of mist crawled over both sides of the chute and collected in the middle. I stared at the roof. Mother Nature waved her wand and the roof turned to vapor and it was suddenly hard to trust that it was there.

Are they coming back? said Sandra.

The helicopter noise was long gone.

I don't know, I said.

I heard her complaining from under the wing. The wing and

the trunk receded behind fog. Her voice was lost in the wind. I came to all fours and stared at my hands, the wet air stuck to them, and I could feel it on my face. It crept under my ski sweater and down my socks, and the wet seemed to bite at my skin. The resurging storm was dark and angry. I was five feet from the wing when I finally saw it again.

I saw a cabin, I said.

They'll come get us, she said.

I huddled against her. Snow piled up fast beyond the edge of the wing and I imagined the well-worn trail back toward my dad evaporating, obliterated by the wind and snow. I stuffed my hands into the cup of my armpits. I looked down to make sure they were there because I could not feel them. The tip of my nose stung and my forehead ached the way it did diving under a chilly winter wave at Topanga.

I turned my back on the cold and buried my face in Sandra's neck. Should we wait here in case they come back? Or should we go?

CHAPTER 16

*I*N THE VILLAGE Dad and I drank water and coconut milk out of the coconuts and ate bananas and more chicken. I gnawed the meat to the bone this time. An elderly woman squeezed aloe vera onto my dad's laceration and he thanked her. We finished everything they gave us and thanked the villagers and went to our hut to hide from the sun.

I could use a siesta, said my dad.

Me too, I said.

We rested on our blankets and I felt the salt on my back and the crusted salt on my eyelashes.

Where do waves come from exactly? I said.

He stared into the dark cone directly above us.

Storms. Wind.

How does it make a wave though?

The storm creates pressure on the ocean. Plunges it kind of, he said. The wind is really strong. Violent. And it drives down into the ocean. Pushing waves out.

And they travel across the ocean?

Yes.

Waves are like a piece of the storm?

That's right, Ollestad.

He turned and the light seeping through the slit washed over his face. We eyed each other, holding on to the beautiful piece of storm.

We were invited to a village gathering that evening. The kids looked at me differently now. And they sat close to me without grabbing me or firing questions at me. We rested on woven mats in a big circle around a fire with pots hanging over it, and they moved the pots with sticks. All the *vaqueros* spoke to my dad now, not just the one with the mustache. I knew my dad was describing the drop-in and the inside of the tube. They kept asking him something over and over and he didn't seem to understand. Then he said, Ah, and stared into the fire and thought about how to say what he wanted to say. He shook his head. He turned to the *vaqueros* and everybody stopped moving or talking. Papaya appeared in her T-shirt and white dress, clean and bright. She sat between two elders and her black eyes were riveted to my dad.

Then she spoke to him, startling me.

He answered her. *Posible.*

One of the *vaqueros* shifted uncomfortably and my dad and Papaya both turned and began speaking to whomever was next to them.

Later when we were eating I whispered to my dad. What were they asking you?

They wanted to know what it was like inside the wave.

What did you say?

I just described what it looked like. But that's not what they meant.

What did they mean?

They meant did I see another world. Spirits and such.

I thought to myself that from the outside we must look like a streaking comet in the drape of the wave.

The girl said it best, whispered my dad.

What did she say?

She said it was a doorway to heaven.

Oh yeah! I said. Don't you think?

I was in heaven so I guess so, said Dad.

The razor-sharp reef flashed across my mind.

But you could get crushed and shredded, I said. Maybe even die.

That's life, Ollestad.

I turned and stared at the flames. Beautiful things were sometimes mixed up with treacherous things, they could even happen at the same time, or one could lead to the other, I thought.

We ate fish and Papaya kept looking at me. Her dark eyes were impossible to interpret. I could not tell if she was pleased or angry. She said something to one of the elders and they turned and looked at me too. I got jumping beans in my stomach, and I hoped she might talk to me. If not tonight then tomorrow, and maybe since she was older she would kiss me and I wouldn't have to kiss her.

Then the youngest *vaquero* said something to her and she began talking with him.

Let's hit the hay, Ollestad, said my dad.

We thanked everyone and went to our hut.

I wonder what her name is? I said, half asleep.

Who?

The pretty girl.

It was dark but I knew he was giving me a goading look. Shit why did I say pretty?

Esperanza, he said.

How do you know?

One of the old ladies told me.

Where's her family?

Her mother and father both died.

How?

I think they got sick, he said.

We surfed under heavy-bellied clouds in the dawn. The surf was smaller and I got a lot of short tubes. With each the purifying sensation carved itself deeper.

My dad went to check out the truck with the older *vaquero* and the youngest *vaquero*. I put on flip-flops and took off with a gang of kids. They captured a huge iguana and we towed it by a vine around its neck and sometimes it tried to run, jerking against the collar. They showed me a cave and we watched the bats hanging upside down, sleeping. They mimed how the bats swooped down on the cows and sucked their blood.

When all the kids went in for their siestas I rested on my blanket and fell asleep also.

After my dad woke me up and made me drink water I noticed there was a dent in the head of the guitar case. My dad saw me eyeing it and he opened it. He pulled out the guitar and there was a ding on the headstock. I thought of the gunshot.

He strummed the guitar, said it still played, put the guitar away, and said he was going to paddle out. I was tired and the sun was high so I stayed in the hut.

I kept thinking about Esperanza, holding hands with her, even kissing her. But my pleasure was undercut by a yearning to leave. I wanted to get to Grandma and Grandpa's or get home. The crisscrossing desires tied me into a foul mood.

My dad returned with a big grin.

Old cowboy Ernesto rode to town to get a mechanic, he said. He should be back pretty soon. And maybe tomorrow the truck will be fixed.

Why don't you know how to fix cars? I said.

I was never interested in that kind of stuff, he said.

Well you should know.

He laughed.

You should, I said.

Think about all the good things, Ollestad. That'll make you feel better.

When we arrived for dinner Ernesto sat by the fire next to his wife and three kids. He appeared worried or upset and my dad spoke to him and he spoke back in short curt sentences. My dad went to our hut and returned with some paper bills, pesos. Ernesto refused them and my dad dropped them in an empty clay bowl. Ernesto spoke to his wife and she took the money out of the bowl and walked to our hut and then came back empty-handed. My dad opened his hands.

Lo siento, he said.

No one spoke around the fire. The elders passed down the

bowls. My dad handed me a bowl and it smelled like pork. I thought about the pigs around back. I was so hungry that I ate it anyway.

Esperanza appeared from the center hut and sat between the elders and ate. Her hair was in a braid and without the thick mane around her face her eyes looked as big as walnuts. Her beauty stood out even more tonight. Like it didn't fit with the humble people of the village and their hardships and silence. She seemed destined for somewhere else. In the firelight her beauty seemed dangerous. I inhaled her sweet aroma. *You will always be Papaya to me.*

Ernesto and the other *vaqueros* finished first and stole away into the main hut with a lantern. My dad repeatedly glanced at the hut aglow from the lantern. Then Ernesto came out and he stared at my dad. My dad stood and went to him. They spoke in quiet voices. My dad nodded. Ernesto nodded. Then he went back into the hut.

My dad sat down beside me and his face was drawn.

What's wrong, Dad?

They're worried that the *federales* will find out they've been helping us.

How'd they find out about the *federales*?

In town I guess.

I thought you said the *federales* would never find us?

They won't. Not while we're here. But later. They may figure it out and hassle everyone.

Are they pissed? I said.

Yeah.

Is that why you tried to give him money?

He nodded.

I thought they just wanted money.

Not these kind of people.

He rubbed his palms together. He only did that when he was thinking really hard. I got scared.

He saw it in my face and put his arm around my shoulder and smiled.

Ollestad. It's okay. *No problemo.*

What are we going to do?

I saw Papaya watching me and I realized my face was pinched, on the verge of tears. I buried my face in the crook of my elbow.

Tomorrow we're going to leave, said Dad. Before you know it we'll be in Vallarta with Grandma and Grandpa, surfin' Sayulita. No sweat.

My face was buried in the crook of my elbow and I was shaking my head wildly. He rubbed my back and my dread turned to anger. Not only could we get kicked out of the village and who knows what else—end up starving in a Mexican jail—but I had ruined everything I had gained with Papaya by falling apart in front of her.

All eyes were on us, so I got myself together. I sat up straight and breathed evenly. Dad handed me a coconut. I drank it because I wanted to be agreeable, as if that would make our circumstances agreeable. My dad stood up and said he'd be right back.

Papaya collected the bowls from the kids and I avoided looking at her. No one spoke and it was somber around the fire. The *vaqueros* came out of the hut and each drank from a coconut, as was their custom.

Then my dad appeared with his guitar. I bristled. How could he be so stupid as to believe they wanted to hear him play and sing? The lying gringo! He sat down, fitting the guitar's curve between his thighs and leaning over the instrument while he strummed flamenco. My arm lurched out to stop him, but it felt like a betrayal and I ended up only petting the air. My dad began to sing in Spanish and Ernesto hardened his eyes and studied my dad's fingers. I stared at the pink fire-lit dirt and hoped it would end soon.

The song came to a fluttering close. Total silence. My embarrassment was amplified by the twinkle in my dad's eye. The *vaqueros* looked fed up. I was ready to make a run for it and looked to my dad for a sign.

Impervious he curled around the guitar and began to strum anew.

Dad, I implored.

He ignored me and began to sing.

I leaned in closer.

Dad . . .

He closed his eyes and continued to sing in Spanish. That's when I caught Papaya staring at my dad's shoulder and neck. Drops of sweat percolated on his skin and glinted in the firelight. She slid her half-veiled eyes toward the fire seamlessly, as if they had been looking there all along. My dad was oblivious and he sang in a booming voice and I checked to make sure the *vaqueros* weren't approaching. One of the elders joined in and the youngest *vaquero* looked bewildered.

At the end of the song everybody except the *vaqueros* clapped. I was astonished by what I had witnessed—my dad had taken the only thing he had, a guitar, and axed his way through adversity. I marveled at his spontaneity, his grace under pressure, the way he transformed the situation—bleak and irreversible—into something beautiful.

My dad sang a few more songs and near the end of the last one he stood up and trailed away toward our hut, his music fading with him. When he called out *Buenos noches*, I got up and went after him.

. . .

We rested on our blankets.

Is everything okay now? I said.

Yep, he said.

A rush of jealousy took me off guard. As awed as I was with Dad, suddenly I wanted to tell him that Papaya was bored—she ignored your fingers plucking the strings, your fancy Spanish lyrics, the sweat on your skin.

What? said my dad.

I didn't say anything, I said—so bitterly that it made him ask if I was feeling okay.

I rolled away from him without responding. I couldn't do the amazing things he could do. I could never have Papaya. For an instant I wondered if that was the real reason that the villagers were pissed off, that he had done something with Papaya. Imagine being so nimble, so charismatic, that there was nothing anyone would ever put past you. I rolled even farther away and slept on the dirt.

At dawn we scoped out the surf and it was clean. The waves were too small for my dad but he hooted after each ride anyway. He never gets bummed about things the way I do, I thought as we drifted on our boards waiting for a set wave. He always finds something cool, some little treasure. That's why everyone—including girls—likes him.

I rode on the back of my dad's saddle. He carried his guitar in one hand and I carried my suitcase. We followed Ernesto along the trail. All the mud had dried in slabs, burying the smaller plants here and there, and I thought we were pretty tough—as opposed to lucky—to have made it that day when we arrived in the storm. After five minutes of bouncing it felt like the suitcase was going to tug my arm out of the shoulder socket. I thought about Dad always seeing the beauty in things and instead of complaining I said,

Wow. So many kinds of green in the jungle.

Dad glanced back at me, more curious than impressed.

The tarp had dried in a messy crinkle. Mud encased all four wheels of the truck and the chassis was flush to the ground. The washing machine's bulge made me realize that I had completely forgotten the original cause for our journey to Mexico.

Ernesto tied the horses to the bumper. My dad put the truck in neutral and Ernesto hawed the horses. Their great necks drove them forward. Haw. Haw. When the wheels cracked free they spit tiles of mud across the trail. Ho. Ho. The horses reared and stamped their feet.

The mechanic appeared, walking down the trail with a toolbox and a crowbar.

What's that thing for? I said, pointing at the crowbar.

I don't know, said my dad.

The mechanic wore a collared shirt and jeans and sandals and he spoke to Ernesto and my dad listened. The mechanic got under the truck and went to work. He chopped at the undercarriage with the crowbar and mud cakes sprayed out from under the truck. My dad handed tools to the mechanic and took them back from the mechanic. Every few minutes Ernesto rode up the trail to check the highway, worried about *federales* I guessed. I swatted mosquitoes and was careful not to complain.

An hour later my dad started the truck and drove it a few

feet forward, then turned it off and got out. He peeled off several paper bills and the mechanic took them and said nothing and left. My dad put the guitar and my suitcase in the cabin and locked the door. He helped me onto the horse and we followed Ernesto back to the village.

It started to rain late in the afternoon so my dad went to talk to Ernesto about leaving sooner rather than later. I wondered where Papaya was and I walked up and down the dirt path saying *Adios* to the kids and their mothers, all the while looking for Papaya.

My dad returned on horseback led by the youngest *vaquero*. I handed my dad the surfboards and he set them across his lap. I got my foot in the stirrup and he helped me up. He waved and thanked everyone and they all waved back without speaking. I waved and hoped to spot Papaya. *Nada*. We trotted into the jungle and something squeezed my heart. I wondered if my dad had said good-bye to her secretly.

The rain was steady and weak and when we reached the truck the ground was beginning to soften. My dad spoke to the *vaquero* and he waited and my dad started the truck and drove forward. The tires only dimpled the ground. The traction was fine. My dad thanked the *vaquero* and he actually smiled and shook my dad's hand. Then my dad's horse followed the *vaquero* around a bend in the trail.

We have to wait until dark. Right? I said.

Yep.

We stood there and he handed me water and I chugged it down. My dad dug his toe into the softening dirt. There sneaked in the notion that if the rain got much harder we might get stuck again, and even if we made it onto the highway it would be hard to see. Then his head moved as if remembering something. He reached into his pocket.

She made this for you.

He handed me a puka-shell necklace. I slipped it over my head. The shells were cool on the back of my neck.

We stood under the drizzle and let the mist coat our faces.

When we came out of the jungle backward and jolted up the embankment and reversed onto the highway it was pitch-black beyond the headlight beams and raining hard. My dad rolled down the window and stuck his head out and we crept along slowly. At the first sharp turn in the road the slashing rain took the shape of a roadblock and I gasped and my dad hit the brakes.

God dang it, Ollestad.

Sorry, I said.

We went through a dark little town made of corrugated tin. An hour passed and there was nothing except the edges of the jungle and the rain splattering on the road. I finally relaxed.

We spent the night in Sayulita, sleeping in the truck. As the sun rose we entered Vallarta and my dad got a little tense. He slouched in his seat and his eyes shifted from side to side. I pretended not to notice. The truck chattered over the cobble-stones and it was weird to see cement buildings, a soccer sta-dium, churches and shops. We crossed the bridge and I knew we were close.

My dad floored it up the steep cobblestone road to my grand-parents' house. The house clung to the hillside and overlooked the entire Vallarta bay. We parked in front of the open garage where the sign CASA NORMAN was screwed into the stone wall. My dad looked at me. He twisted his lips to one side.

Well that was quite a journey. Wasn't it? he said.

I nodded.

Maybe we don't want to scare Grandma and Grandpa, you know? he added.

He patted my leg. He looked in the rearview and brushed down his mustache with his fingers. He hadn't shaved in days and his whiskers poked out, gray ones appearing.

You got some blond surfer hairs, I said, thinking I was awfully clever repeating back to him one of his own jokes.

He smiled and then Grandma came out of the house.

There was a lot of kissing and hugging and she was ecstatic about the new washing machine. My dad said it was *no problemo* and talked about my great tube rides. Grandma took a deep breath, put her hand on her chest and lifted onto her toes.

Oh my, she said.

Grandpa came home and kissed us all and he and my dad carried the washing machine up some stairs, grunting and groaning until they got the machine onto the deck above the garage and Grandpa hooked it up. Grandpa knew how to fix things because he used to be a telephone repairman. He could climb a pole faster than any other man in his unit, only missing one day of work in thirty years. Thinking of him shimmying up the pole reminded me that he was a great dancer like Dad. That's how he had wooed Grandma, dazzling her with his waltz and swing moves. He married Grandma after her first husband left her with two kids—Uncle Joe and Aunt Charlotte. Grandpa was willing to take on a preformed family, which was rare in those days, said Grandma. Then my dad was born and, last, his sister Aunt Kristina.

We all went swimming, then after dinner we played a card

game. Grandma asked me about my puka-shell necklace. Already what had happened seemed like a dream in another time long ago.

I found the shells where I got tubed, I said. Somebody strung them for me.

They sound like wonderful people, she said. That's Mexico.

For dessert we had apples that had been brought down from California by one of the many visitors my grandparents took in each month. Dad bit into a worm and Grandma got excited.

Great, Norie. Now we know they're organic, she said.

After the card game, Grandma wrote the *Mexico Report*, a monthly update sent to the entire family. But Bob Barrow and my mom said that it was the occasional letter by Grandpa that proved he should have been writing the report, and Al said that Grandpa's letters reminded him of Hemingway.

It was a real luxury to sleep on a soft mattress that night. I slept in a separate room, hearing the bugs buzzing and the animals thrashing around, and I wasn't scared at all.

My dad had arranged a special treat for me. We went to the airport the next day and Chris Rohloff, my friend who I surfed with at Topanga, stepped off the plane.

You bought him a ticket? I said.

Well you said you missed your friends.

Grandpa and Dad took us surfing every day, driving Grandpa's orange jeep. In Sayulita Grandpa would order *ostras* from the only restaurant in the village while we waxed up the boards. The waiter would write down the order, take off his shirt and then drive his boat out to the rocky headland. When we came in from the surf the oysters would be waiting for us under the *palapa*.

Finally having a buddy of my own to surf and pal around with instead of my dad gave me a taste of what pure fun was like. There was no one pressing for more. I loved when Rohloff and

I just hung out, sometimes letting good waves go by while we made up our own surfing lingo like *tweak-mondo* and *hairball-McGulicutty*.

One day we rode burros up to a waterfall and all four of us had a contest: who could swim under the waterfall and back the fastest. It was tricky because the current tried to sweep you into the boulders and tried to tow you into the rapids just below our pool. After Dad and Grandpa clearly let us boys win the contest, declaring a tie, Dad dove off the top of the waterfall. Grandpa spotted a deep hole in the pool for him to land in. I could tell that Rohloff thought my dad was the coolest guy in the world, and it made me proud. Too bad it only lasted a week, I thought when Rohloff boarded the plane home.

CHAPTER 17

F ROM AN ELEVATED position above the crash site I could see Sandra and myself under the wing of the airplane. We were fused together. An ice-clad heap. Frosted hair. Blue lips. It took me a while to understand that I was dreaming. I felt like I was swimming and swimming and swimming. Never reaching the top. Running out of oxygen. A last gulp of air trapped in my throat.

Yielding to the warm water I sank. A pebble landing softly on a cushioned floor. Safe. Comfortable. Warm at last.

I saw this as if from outside my body and finally realized I had to pull myself out of the sleep. Move your arm, lift your head, I told myself. I used all my strength but to no avail. Instead I waded in blobs of glue. Drunk and unable to coordinate my muscles. The feathery bottom was irresistible. Cozy and inviting.

No. Get up, I insisted.

I bucked. My lids cracked, then closed again under pneumatic pressure.

Now my fingers wiggled. They are wiggling. Or I just think they are—a dream within a dream within a dream. No they are wiggling. And then a vacuum of bliss drew me deep into a heated cave. I countered the seductive sleep by trying to move my fingers again.

One eye splintered open. Light. White. Cool. But dark warmth enveloped me once more. Mmm. Goodnight.

I ordered my fingers to spread. A pitchfork. Elbow unbend. Elbow unbend. Unbend!

My arm was reaching up. But it would hit the wing. I see from my elevated perch that I am only dreaming this. Reach, I urge. Punch the wing.

My fingers struck metal.

Pull open your eyelids. Use anything. I used my stomach muscles. My forehead muscles.

The lids peeled open and my hand banged against the metal roof. All was blurry and I lunged toward the light. Don't close your fucking eyes, Ollestad.

My body corkscrewed as if wringing itself out. I was in the snow. My eyelids dipped and then ripped free of the last tugging webs of sleep. I saw the snow and the tree and the wing. It was darker now and that accentuated my panic—afternoon is here, next is night, no chance then.

The horror of having observed myself slipping away widened my focus, allowing my dad's crumpled body, the pilot's leaky brains, and the wound in Sandra's forehead to assault me. I wanted to roll back under the wing and say good night to this cruel hell.

Fight through it, Ollestad, boomed a voice. Keep moving.

I shouted under the wing.

Get up!

Sandra did not flinch.

I reached under the wing and shook her violently.

Get up! You can't sleep.

Norman?

Get up.

I'm tired, Norman. Very tired.

I know, but you can't sleep. My dad said when you freeze to death you feel warm and then you fall asleep and never wake up.

Her head moved toward me and I saw that her eyes were wide open. She was staring at me but was focused somewhere else.

Big Norm is dead, she said.

The bad thoughts tried to get me. I lolled my head and arched my shoulders.

We have to go now, I said.

They're coming.

They're not coming.

She stared at me. I studied the wound caving in one side of her forehead by her hairline, her dislocated shoulder that made one arm dangle like a partially severed branch. She receded farther under the wing, as if to hide this from me, and her eyes dimmed and her face looked like a skull.

Sandra. We have to go, I said.

No.

I'm going, I said.

You can't leave me here.

Then come on.

I waited. Scoped out the conditions. Heavy snow falling. Now there's going to be a layer of snow dust over the ice. It'll be really difficult to tell where the *grippier* snow is. Shit. How will we hold on? Especially Sandra.

I reached up and touched the branches sheltering me. Some

of the branches were stiffer than others. I broke off two long stems, then snapped off as many twigs and needles as I could. My hands were frozen again and my dexterity was awkward.

We have to go now, I called to her.

I kneeled down to see under the wing. She was squirming, her good arm oaring her forward like a bird flopping along the ground dragging a broken limb.

Sandra emerged from under the wing. Her eyes lolled in their trenches and the skin around them strained as if trying to compose the landscape.

It's icy, I said. Use this like an ice axe. Okay?

I illustrated by jabbing the stem into the snow and tugging on it.

I can't use my arms, she said.

Use that arm.

I handed her the stem. She gripped it and held it up to her face like a baby pondering a toy she didn't understand.

I'll go below you. Use me to step on, I said. Stay right above me so I can stop you from sliding. Okay?

Fuckin' hell.

Okay?

Your face is cut open, she said.

I touched my face. Felt around. Traced frozen blood over a gash in my chin. Another gash on my cheek.

It's not bleeding, I said.

Am I okay? she said.

You're fine. Let's go.

CHAPTER 18

M Y DAD AND I took the ferry directly from Puerto Vallarta to La Paz, avoiding any chance of running across those *federales* again. From La Paz we drove the Baja highway north, homebound. In Tijuana we went to a bullfight. I rooted for the bull.

We spent the night in a hotel in San Diego and the next morning my dad woke me and we were in front of my mom's house on Topanga Beach. He opened the door to the side walkway and I listened for sounds of Nick coming down the corridor. My dad knocked on the sliding-glass door.

Hey hey, said my mom as she opened the door. It's the Dynamic Duo.

I peeked inside. She leaned down and kissed me.

Hi Mom, I said.

Look at you. Brown as a berry.

My dad stepped inside and went to the fridge. My mom patted the back of my head.

So blond, Norman, she said. How was the trip?

Good, I said.

My dad bit into a peach and he shut the fridge and peered at me over Mom's shoulder. In his eyes not a trace of those rifle barrels or the gunshot or the days we spent adrift—just the afterglow of tube rides and sunshine.

So it wasn't as bad as you thought it was going to be? she said.

I shook my head.

It wasn't until dinnertime that I asked about Nick.

He's away for a few weeks, said my mom.

I switched on the TV to my favorite show, *All in the Family*, and we watched it while we ate. When the first commercial came on I turned around and looked at my mom. No bruise, no scratch, exactly the same as the other eye.

It was quiet around the house for the rest of August. My mom didn't have to teach for a few weeks and I just hung around Topanga and skateboarded and surfed and played with Charley and Sunny. Everybody on the beach was talking about eminent domain and I gathered the county or the state, somebody, was trying to kick us off the beach. Someone said they could do it because we didn't own the land, just the houses. That seemed impossible.

Hockey camp filled my weekend mornings and football practice filled my weekday afternoons and I alternated my nights among my mom, my dad and Eleanor. Eleanor was the only one

I talked to about Nick and my mom. She mostly asked me questions, and I liked how she listened carefully to my answers.

One night Eleanor and I were in her kitchen preparing dinner. She asked me how I felt when Nick called me a failure and a liar and such, or when my dad made me get up at four in the morning to go to hockey practice. I didn't like it of course, I told her. Then her husband Lee opened the front door, walked in and set a broom against the cabinet, heading for the bedroom.

Where's the rest, honey? said Eleanor.

What do you mean? said Lee.

The chicken and the salad dressing.

You never said anything about getting chicken, said Lee.

You think I wanted you to go to the market at nine o'clock at night to buy a broom?

Well. I thought it was kind of strange.

They stood watching each other. They were both very small people, very gentle and sensitive. So they studied one another as if trying to feel the other out.

Lee, said Eleanor. It took you forty-five minutes to buy a broom?

I wanted to get the exact right one for you, Eleanor, he said.

Like gas leaking from a balloon laughter seeped out of my mouth. I couldn't control it and I threw back my head, surrendering. Eleanor was next, then Lee, and soon the three of us were keeled over in the kitchen.

Lee said he was exhausted from the laughing and had to go lie down. Eleanor prepared dinner. While boiling the spaghetti she explained to me about *bad pretends* and *good pretends*.

You have a choice, Norman. You don't have to believe Nick's bad stories. Those are his bad pretends about what may or may not happen, she said. You can make up your own good stories. Good pretends.

But then it's just made up, I said.

So are the bad stories, she said. They're about Nick. They're not really about you.

That's not fair, I said.

No it isn't, she said.

Eleanor probably sensed I was getting overwhelmed and announced that dinner was finally ready.

We got into bed with Lee and watched a TV movie and ate spaghetti. I did not comprehend every nuance of the *pretends* concept, but it made me recall a photograph of Nick wearing a military uniform, from one of those military schools I assumed. He was strikingly handsome and he looked like he knew it. Maybe he's the one that woke up one day realizing that the world did not revolve around him, I thought, and he's having a bad pretend that the same will happen to me.

On Sunday I wandered down to Barrow's to get a longboard. A bunch of boards poked over the rotted wood fence where the outdoor shower was, next to Barrow's deck on which poker was played almost every weekend, rain or shine. I was hoping to spot the red board that was already dinged up so I wouldn't have to worry about it hitting the rocks at low tide. As I angled up the sandbank, Sandra and my dad appeared, stepping out of the window-door onto the deck. I stopped below the sandbank because they were holding hands. She was back, and I knew there would be no explanation from my dad.

My dad sat down at the poker table and Sandra rubbed his neck while he got his poker chips. I changed my mind and took Sunny up the creek to my fort.

. . .

A week later I came home from football practice and my mom was taping together cardboard boxes.

Well, she said. We finally lost.

You mean we have to move for sure?

Yep. The state won. They're kicking us off the beach.

There was a big party the following weekend and Nick came home. Everyone on the beach gathered at the yellow submarine house where Trafton, Woody, Shane and Clyde lived. Trafton and Clyde's band, Blue Juice, played and everyone danced. Sandra wore a green silk bandanna and a white miniskirt and no top. I watched her dance and I compared Papaya's slow rhythm and long banana-shaped eyelids to Sandra's hardened expression. Even their breasts were opposites, Papaya's so round and plump compared to Sandra's torpedoes.

Later I got a hot dog and Nick tended the barbecue with his shirt off. His neck and face were red and his body was pale.

Life is a long series of readjustments, he said. Remember how I said you need to be prepared?

I nodded.

Well this is what I meant. And there's more of it coming, he said. You understand?

Yeah it's like when it's all sunny and you're skiing and by the afternoon it's snowing and freezing cold. You gotta adjust to it, I said.

Nick's eyebrows perked up and he opened his palms toward the sky and stretched his arms out. Right on the money, he said.

I moved along before he could bring up the skateboarding lie. I found my mom dancing with our neighbors, Wheeler and Maggie. Next to them boogied Sandra and my dad. I sat on a rock and watched the action.

Late that afternoon the wind died and the ocean glassed over and I paddled out with my dad. It was small and we were the only two surfers in the water.

Well you're getting your wish, Ollestad.

How?

I bought a house in the Palisades for you and your mom. I got a great deal on it, Ollestad.

Right on. Does it have a pool?

No pool.

Doesn't matter. I can bike around and go to friends' houses like every day.

Yep. But one day you'll miss old Topanga Beach. You were born here.

I looked over the backs of the waves and followed a roller-rink curve of sand past Barrow's deck, then back along the beach. Dogs moved in packs, Sunny chased a stick, Carol walked her llama by leash around the point, Jerry did wheelies on his dirt bike, and the dancing bodies weaved together like a parachute undulating to the music.

My dad put his hand on my back, as if to connect us, and we watched Topanga Beach for the last time. A set came and he told me to go. We rode those stained-glass waves lit from behind by the dying orange sun until dark.

My father

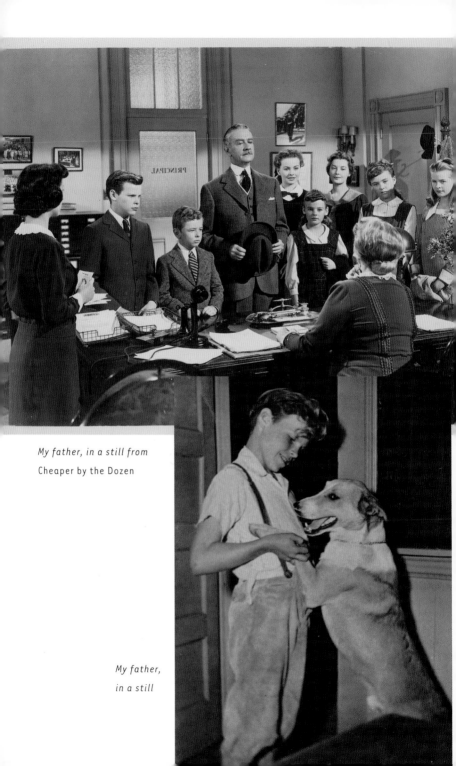

My father, in a still from
Cheaper by the Dozen

My father,
in a still

A BOLD AND DARING REPORT BY A FORMER AGENT OF THE FEDERAL BUREAU OF INVESTIGATION...

INSIDE THE FBI

BY NORMAN OLLESTAD

Dad at the office

My father's book,
Inside the FBI

My mom and dad

Dad and Al Freedman with Austrian woman at The Castle in Feldkirk, Austria

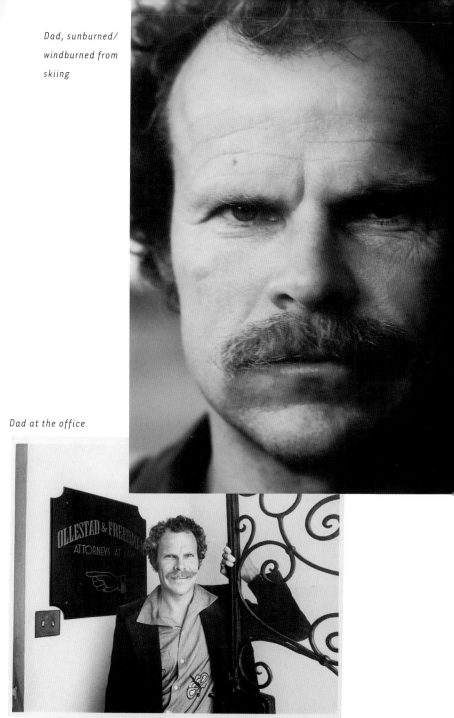

Dad, sunburned/
windburned from
skiing

Dad at the office

St. Anton, Austria

Our family

First surfboard. All shots are on Topanga Beach

Surfing with Dad and Christian Andersen

Surfing with Dad

Dad

With Mom and Dad

Puerto Vallarta

St. Anton

St. Anton

Ski race in the U.S.

With Mom—same pair of blue Vans I wore February 19, 1979

At grandparents' house, Puerto Vallarta, Mexico

CHAPTER 19

*T*HE TERRAIN BELOW the big tree seemed like the easiest way down. It was less slick than the funnel on the far side of the chute where my dad was. I crouched below Sandra and told her to do the same.

Get the stick into the snow, I said. Chop it in every time you slip.

I kept the heel of my palm under her leather sole and with my other hand I checked down the first few inches of the chute with the stick. She remained clinging to the slope face like a salamander.

Okay. Inch down to me, I said.

She let go and barreled into my outstretched hand. My stick ripped out of the snow and we both starting sliding. I dug with my toes and raked both hands into the snow. I was slowing down and I used my shoulder and the side of my head to cradle Sandra's boots. Luckily the snow was soft enough for me to maneuver us to a standstill. The stick was in my hand when I looked, unable to be sure just by touch.

You have to use the stick to ease down! I said. Don't lift it all the way up. Okay?

It's hard. I feel funny, Norman, she said. Is there something wrong with my head?

No. Just hang in there. We're almost down.

How many times had my dad used the same exact line on me? I thought.

I stole a glimpse of the chute below. It fell and fell—fifty feet, a thousand feet, I did not know. My lie would be revealed soon, and I wondered what I would say next to encourage Sandra.

Then I realized that we had traversed across the chute toward the dreaded funnel. The whole chute slanted that way, as if tilted. So I arranged Sandra on my right shoulder to balance against the leftward pull into the funnel.

Okay, I said.

We crept down and I used my foot like a rudder, pushing against the slant of the chute, trying to keep us on the softer, bumpier terrain. As we descended I peered downward to get a bearing and felt Sandra lose contact with me. When I looked up she was creeping toward the funnel. Her stick turned outward so that it only grazed the crust.

Get the stick down! I yelled. Turn your hand down!

First it went up and then down and she continued to gain speed. She was about to really take off across the chute, I knew, so I scuttled as fast as I could sideways and downward. Ten feet away loomed the funnel—a threshold we could not cross. Her body jolted as if kicking into another gear, so I took a chance and pushed off, falling sideways like a spaceman until I was beneath her.

She butted against my shoulder and head—the only way to

absorb her weight and still get my fingers into the ice. I propped onto my toes and kicked in. For no logical reason the snow was pulpier here and gradually I found traction. We stopped just before the terrain curled into the funnel. We had no more chances left.

You have to slide *straight* down, Sandra. Understand?

My arm is getting tired, Norman.

She sounded weak and that humbled me.

Just a little more, I said. You can do it.

How much further?

Not much. Ready?

We shouldn't have left, she said.

We're almost down. Ready?

God please save us, she said.

I hadn't thought about God. If we get down then I'll believe in God, I told myself.

I realized that my fingers and feet were completely numb now and that I would not be able to handle Sandra's weight much longer.

I drew the stick to my hip, plunking it into the crust. I bent my knees, detaching from Sandra's feet.

Stay with me, I said.

My free hand reached low and sunk to my wrist. My fingers rummaged for a stake in the ice. One leg stretched and the toe kneaded the top layer, kicking in, testing the hold. Then the other foot performed the same ritual. We moved down methodically and I felt like I was getting my technique wired.

We're golden, I said, using one of my dad's favorite sayings. Keep it going.

I looked upslope—my words drawing me back to him. I saw the sapling tree cricked over from my earlier fall. We've only gone thirty feet, I realized. We'll never make it at this pace.

Never. When I glimpsed my dad way above the tree, a sketched figure, I innately understood that I had to squash the doubt curdling inside me.

This never-ending ice curtain was all in the way you chose to see it, like *water-juice.*

We gotta hustle, I said to Sandra. We're in like Flynn though.

I inched lower and at first she stayed with me. My shoulder was numbing and I was so focused on my own movements that soon I was five feet below her.

Straight down to me, I coaxed her. *No problemo.*

Instead of moving downward Sandra's body tracked left. I couldn't climb upward to stop her. Her left hand eased over the funnel's threshold and just like that my plan went to shit. Sandra's arm, shoulder then hip slipped into the funnel.

CHAPTER 20

*B*EFORE *I KNEW* it I had started the sixth grade. Grammar school was walking distance from my new house, a two-bedroom, two-bath 1940s Craftsman built on a bluff overlooking Santa Monica Bay. My dad got a great deal on it because a few years back during a big rainstorm the house next door had slid into the canyon. My dad believed our house was safe because it had been tested by the big storm and survived.

Right away I was taken off guard by my new suburban life. Most of my peers' references and quips involved video games, baseball cards and knowing the latest happenings of *Starsky and Hutch*, all stuff I was unfamiliar with. So I made it my goal to learn how to play Outer Space and watch more *Starsky and Hutch*.

Within days it became painfully obvious that swearing was frowned upon and that my stories of Mexico or Topanga Beach were hardly endearing me to the neighborhood kids. They just looked at me like I was crazy, and kept me out of their conversations. And my cozy picture of walking to school with my friends was abruptly altered by the new desegregation busing law. I did get to walk along the sidewalk with my neighbors, as I had fantasized, but when we got to school we had to board a bus and drive forty minutes to South Central Los Angeles.

Some things stayed exactly the same. Nick sat in the same rocking chair watching the same news programs. My mom picked fights with him every once in a while and Sunny slept in my room. I spent my weekends on Topanga Beach surfing with the legends. Most of them had moved up the canyon or right across the highway into the Snake Pit. We all congregated around the lifeguard station (my former neighbor's house that had been converted into a lifeguard station), storing our boards in its shade, hiding our coveted bars of wax in its nooks and crannies. The beach was strange now, just a stretch of dirty sand and broken stairs leading to nothing.

That fall Nick filmed all my Saturday-morning football games. Later in the week he would bring the Super 8 reels to the coach's house and sometimes the team would meet there and the coach would critique our plays. On game days Nick would lend me his heavy fishing weights for me to stuff under my thigh pads and into my jockey cup during the weigh-in with the refs. I was the only kid in the whole league trying to weigh more than he actually did. Half of my team spent the morning in a sauna trying to lose a couple pounds so they could play. Nick was my biggest fan, cheering from the bleachers where he filmed. He told all his friends how I went head-to-head with the biggest kids and never backed down. It felt good to impress him and I wished we always got along so well. But I never knew when Nick was going to explode again, and a part of me was always braced for it, and that made it hard to trust those sweet moments.

My dad made all the games too, but never said much about

them. He had damaged one of his knees playing football in high school and thought football was not worth jeopardizing hockey, skiing and surfing—sports that I had a real chance to excel in.

Winter came early and before Thanksgiving I was training with the Mount Waterman ski team—four members strong. At the end of one long day of racing gates my dad made me ski the sheer ice face back to the car. He made me ski it two more times so that I'd learn ice.

On Thanksgiving Day I skied the Cornice at Mammoth, dreaded for its ten- to fifteen-foot lip hanging over the run. It was treacherous dropping in, intermittently airborne while slicing across the wind-buffed overhang. According to my dad it was good for me so we skied it all day.

On the drive home my dad was suffering from the malaria he had contracted while working for Project India back in the '50s. It often made him feel drowsy and he told me he was going to *rest one eye*. As I had done several times before, I took the wheel while his foot kept even pressure on the pedal. If a car appeared up ahead I was to wake him up even though he was supposedly just *resting one eye*. It never struck me as dangerous. In fact it seemed like a good deal because when he woke from his catnap he always felt *fantastic* and I was always proud to share the load.

I finished my homework just in time to watch *All in the Family*. My mom cooked steak, serving it with brown rice and salad with walnuts and avocados. Nick came home and interrupted our show so he could watch some news special. He ate his steak with both hands and shoveled down the rice with the large serving spoon.

Near the end of the special he turned to me.

Stop chomping your food, he said.

I slowed my chewing and made sure to keep my mouth closed so no sounds would escape. During the first commercial Nick recited an article he had read about manners and how if they weren't learned young they became an embarrassing indiscretion when you got older.

No more eating with your hands or chomping your food, he declared.

Look at *you*, Nick, said my mom.

I'm talking about Norman. Don't make excuses for him.

Where do you think he gets his bad habits?

You're right, he said. But now it's time to get control of the situation.

I was struck by how it sounded like an emergency and I wondered how he would have reacted when I was upside down in that tree well or sliding down that icy face or drowning in ten-foot surf. Real emergencies.

My mom made me a cup of ice cream with chocolate sauce. I ate it while we watched a sit-com and Nick had his first vodka.

Goddamn it, Norman, he said after a few minutes.

My hand stopped mid-spoon. My mouth was open. I had been slurping.

Sorry, I said.

Go in the den.

I won't do it again. I'm sorry. I just want to watch the end.

He grabbed my arm and the cup and walked me into the den. He slammed down the cup and jammed me into the chair.

If you can't control your slurping then you eat separately, he said. Until you learn.

I wasn't hungry anymore so I went downstairs to my room. My whole body shivered. I turned on the furnace and got into bed and buried myself head-to-toe under the blanket.

The very next day on the way to the bus one of the neighborhood gang pointed out another kid in our grade named Timothy. I recognized Timothy as the boy who always looked down
at his feet, muttered, sat alone, read comic books at recess, and
startled easily. He reminded me of a beaten dog—sort of how I
felt last night. One of the gang called to him across the street.

Hey, Creepothy, he yelled and the other boys laughed.

Timothy did not look up. He turned away from us, stopping
so that we'd get far ahead of him. I kept glancing back at him,
fascinated. He was skittish like me, but he couldn't hide it. He
probably has a mean dad or stepfather, I thought. I wanted to
cross the street and walk with him. Then the idea repulsed me.
I was the first one to walk ahead.

Later that week Nick punished me again for chomping and I
sat in the den and ate alone. When I was finished he handed me
a piece of paper.

A contract, he said.

I looked at it, unmoved.

Read it.

I hereby promise to get control of myself and take responsibility for my actions. I will not chomp, slurp or eat with my
mouth open. If I do I will eat alone.

Do you understand it?

I nodded.

Sign it.

I signed it.

A few days later I saw Timothy at recess picking his nose. He
sat on a bench in the corner of the yard. Somebody threw the
kickball at him and he tried to duck it, tripping over his feet. It
bounced off his face as he scurried to the other side of the yard.
I wondered if they'd do the same to me if I stopped being good
at kickball. I played my butt off that day.

CHAPTER 21

SANDRA'S BODY SPILLED into the funnel. The only way to save her was to let myself tack with the slanting chute into the funnel. It would be polished to a slick. I had no edges, no poles, no gloves, just fingers and sneakers. In a flash her slow motion fall would become a toboggan ride to the bottom, wherever that was.

I lifted the stick and my feet, pushing off my right hand into the funnel.

Sandra was above me, plummeting now. I craned outward and her heel rapped my forehead. Then I axed the stick down. My toes dug and my free hand clawed. Under the half-inch of crust it was solid ice. I knew ice. I could ski it as well as any kid around. But there was nothing I could do now. We sailed as if in a free fall.

The chute's overall slant also ran through the funnel. So our momentum ran us across the funnel instead of straight down its gut. Another lucky break. Just below the rocky border was an embankment of snow that was angled in such a way that the snow was softer here. As we careened up the embankment I saw crags of rock and intermittent trees mottling it.

I burrowed one sneaker into the snow and collided with something hard. I bounced off it and felt my trailing arm whack a rock. Fortunately it checked our plummet, slowing us down.

Sandra was directly above me. I grabbed her ankle and hacked at the snow with the stick and fished for another rock with my foot. The stick had broken and wasn't much use. I worked it down my palm to expose more tip. My foot tapped another rock and I rolled my weight onto that side. My toe caught the next crag of rocks, each catch a deceleration, until that foot planted against the blunt face of a larger rock. We came to a stop like a crushed beer can.

Sandra was crying, wailing out. I looked up and her ankle was in my hand yet I could not feel it there. The skin on my first set of knuckles was gone. A pink liquid oozed out.

I studied the larger rocks rising out from the crag of rock we were currently mashed against. How to climb up onto them, the chute's border, and get us out of the funnel? Once atop the spine of rock I visualized us making our way downslope. Each five-foot drop to the next little ledge will be slick with nothing to grip, I thought. Then I saw us tumbling and bouncing down the rocky cascade and that made me abandon that idea.

We have to stay against these rocks, Sandra. See how we can use them to slow down? See? See, the ice is a little softer here. Okay?

Sandra said something about God's wrath. Why is she suddenly so religious? I thought.

Here we go, I said.

Using the softer snow and crags of rock along the embankment, we moved down as a unit. With Sandra's boots crutched on my left shoulder, my head braced her to that side. And miraculously she still had the stick in her good hand.

Over the next few minutes we only slipped once. Right away, I leveraged my shoe tip against a rock, halting us.

Good job keeping your feet against me, I said.

Why are you doing this to us, Norman?

Ask God, I said.

I pulled down her boot soles tight to my left shoulder.

Here we go, I said.

We moved on our stomachs and it got darker from the ashen fog washing over our backs. Fifteen feet lower the embankment grew steeper and we had to fight against sliding back into the funnel.

Then the embankment of snow dissolved into a vertical wall of rocks. I stopped and felt out a tuft-line of pliable snow maybe three inches wide, trailing along the foot of the wall. My numb hands cleaved to this supple thread. I begged the snow-thread to keep trailing downward or we'd be forced into the funnel. With the side of my head I braced Sandra's ankle and we started moving again.

Keep your upper body straight, I said.

Keep your upper body straight, she repeated. Then again as if reminding herself.

We scaled down at a snail's pace. I hoped for the chute to end soon, or for us to come upon a tree growing out of a crack in the rock wall, low enough for us to grab. I needed to rest. But the scenery never changed. The fog pinned us to the thread of snow, our lifeline. A few feet later still nothing had changed. No sign of that wooded section. Just the nasty funnel at our hip. Don't rush, I told myself. Inch at a time. Once you get going there's no stopping.

CHAPTER 22

*O*UR LITTLE WHITE Porsche passed the Mammoth turnoff and kept going north on 395. I sat behind my dad giving him a head massage. Afterward I got in the passenger's seat and we played Muga Booga, speaking crazy languages to each other like cavemen or apes. Then we switched on my dad's new CB radio and talked to some truckers, getting weather reports and smokey sightings. After that we played License Plate and I found the one with the lowest number right before we hit Bridgeport and my dad turned onto a country road.

Where're we going? I said.

It's a surprise.

A ghost town?

He nodded.

Cool.

The town of Bodie was scattered on a mild slope amongst sage, a pale lime in the dry cold of winter. We wandered the barren streets. A lone brick facade seemed to waver in the wind. The other structures were steepled shacks and my dad said up to 10,000 people once lived in this place. I asked all the same questions I always asked when we came to ghost towns.

The gold ran out, Ollestad. They moved on.

Why do we like ghost towns so much, Dad?

He shrugged.

No traffic, he said.

In the morning my dad waxed my skis with the hotel iron.

They keep talking about this kid, he said. Lance McCloud. They say he's the best. Everybody tells me about him.

How old is he?

I don't know. He's a Junior 4 like you. Sometimes he races J3 to test himself against the older kids.

I do that too, right?

Yep. Anything to help you qualify for the Southern Cal Championship race.

When's that? I said.

Little over two months. President's weekend, he said.

Does Uncle Joe still own this hotel? I said.

Yeah.

He ran the iron up and down the base of my skis.

You got to go fast today, he said.

I will.

Why talk about beating the best kid when I have never even beaten the second or third best? I thought.

I don't weigh enough, I said.

He stopped ironing my skis.

Use your technique, he said.

What difference does it make on the flats?

Hey. That's not an excuse.

But I can't go fast 'cause of my weight.

Tuck the flats. Do anything you can.

Tuck slalom gates?

Don't worry about going fast, okay.

But you told me to.

I know, but the wax will take care of that, Ollestad.

He moved the iron onto the second ski.

Why do I pee in my pants every time? I said.

You get excited. Don't worry about that.

But the other kids don't pee in their pants.

How do you know?

Dad put down the iron and set the skis against the wall.

You really want me to beat that kid. Don't you? I said.

He looked at me, his mouth parted. Naw, he said. Don't worry about him.

Why'd you talk about him then?

I don't know. I'm just sick of hearing about him I guess.

Then why talk about him?

Just . . . to get it off my chest, Norman.

He got the scraper out of his bag and shaved the top layer of wax off my bases.

Fourth place, tenth place, first place, he said. That's not what it's about.

But everybody's trying to win, I said.

I know. But we're not. We're just out here to make some good turns. Get a little better each time. We're just out here for the hell of it.

His mustache was unruly, bushing out in all directions, and his eyes looked groggy. He watched me closely, searching my face. I gazed right through him to some place beyond his eyes where his explanations might make sense. I couldn't really understand what he meant by *for the hell of it*.

You don't care? I said.

All I care about is that you keep going, Boy Wonder. Don't get stuck on how you finished last time or the turn you just made. Go after the next one with all you've got.

We signed in with the Heavenly Valley race department and the race official asked where the hell Mount Waterman was.

Los Angeles, said my dad.

That's a long way from Lake Tahoe, said the official. He smiled and handed me a bib. Good luck, he said through his smile.

I was the sole representative of my team so my dad and I slipped the course together, with him acting as my coach. It was a gentle slope with pretty tight gates and powdery snow.

You got 'em in the powder, he said.

I felt the pressure again and it was confusing. It was clear that he wanted me to win no matter what he claimed. He was trying to be sneaky about it—tease me into winning without feeling any stress. I was onto him.

It'll probably stop snowing, I said with spite. No more powder.

Then the ruts will get big, he said. That's no problem for you. You got 'em in the ruts.

I scoffed. Maybe I don't.

He gave me a long look. I had made my point so I kept my mouth shut.

A quarter of the way down he insisted on getting real close to the Heavenly Valley ski team in front of us. My dad would repeat to me what the Heavenly coach told his team and finally the coach addressed my dad.

Excuse me sir. What team are you from?

Mount Waterman, said my dad. The coach couldn't make it so we were hoping to pick up a few pointers.

These kids' families pay a lot of money for ski team. I don't think it's fair for you to get advice for free. Do you?

My dad's jaw muscle flinched. Then he smiled.

I'll pay for it, he said.

You'll have to go work that out with the team president, said the coach.

But you're the coach. You must have authority to decide who can train with the team, said my dad.

No sir.

Let's go, I said.

My dad looked at his watch.

The race is going to start soon, my dad said to the coach.

The coach raised his head as if to get a better look at my dad. My dad leaned onto his poles, settling in. The team behind us appeared at our rear. Then the Heavenly coach shook his head and turned away, addressing his racers.

My dad told me to listen closely to the coach's *inside info*. My head was bent toward the ground and I nodded.

The wind picked up and the snow fell hard and it was difficult to see by the time we got to the bottom. A voice came over the speakers mounted on the night-skiing lampposts.

Due to diminishing visibility the race is delayed until further notice, said the voice.

Son of a bitch, said my dad.

He was pissed, I knew, because he believed I had the advantage in these stormy conditions.

Well. Let's go powder skiing, he said.

. . .

I pointed my head into the wind and we rode several chairs before he led me into the trees. We hiked and he whistled and sang a Tyrolean song I remembered from our trips to St. Anton. We skied a long ridge-spine and the snow was thick and heavy, Sierra Cement they called it because the storms hitting the Sierra Mountains had too much moisture. Every few turns my dad hooted and sang as if it was perfectly light Alta powder.

I followed him down a gully and the snow was awful. I was exhausted by the time we made it to the comeback trail.

One more, said my dad as we schussed along the trail.

No way, I said.

Why not?

The other kids aren't going out of bounds looking for powder, I said. We might miss the race.

Ollestad—we can do it all, he said.

He opened his arms as if offering me the valley and the forest, maybe the entire world.

It was snowing hard and the nightlights finally reached full glow when the course setter announced that the gates would be loosened up a bit because of the conditions. My dad groaned. Among the coaches and parents gathered around the race department, he was the only person unhappy with the decision. My chances were whittling away.

I heard Lance McCloud's name when I got to the starting tent and I circumvented the crowd and finally saw him. He was a small boy like myself and he wore a spiffy ski team suit and all his teammates listened intently as he spoke. His coach sharpened his edges and waxed his skis and I watched him stretching and joking with his friends, comfortable and relaxed. My dad kneeled beside me and reviewed the gates with me, then he looked over my skis like he was going to tune them up but we didn't have any files or wax with us.

Lance raced second and nobody else was close to his time. Finally they called my number and I poled nervously into the starting gate. The starter counted down—five-four-three-two-one-Go!—and I kicked off the pad and broke the wand. Instinctively I banked on two skis into my first turn, powder style. The rut was filled with snow and I felt my skis spring me into the next turn. I sailed through the pillowy ruts as if skiing powder bumps. It was not something I had planned and I questioned what the hell I was doing. But I didn't have to jam the edges and the skis sliced right through each turn, running well.

I crossed the red dye of the finish line and the first thing I saw was Lance McCloud's face, twisted with envy. I knew I had beaten him. Checking the board I had the best time by half of a second. My dad appeared and waved me over.

Pretty good, Ollestad, he said in front of the leering crowd. And we skied away.

We waited in the starting tent for the second run to begin. Lance's team kept their backs to us and whispered to each other. A couple boys from Squaw Valley and Incline Village congratulated me and I thanked them. My dad didn't say a word. The kid who finished twentieth went first. I would go last. My dad hiked over to the starting gate and when he came back he was shaking his head.

What? I said.

They got a whole team of people scraping away the snow in the ruts.

Why?

Why do you think?

Oh, I said, understanding that it was for Lance. He must not like powder.

When it was Lance's turn the tent got real quiet. I was right behind him and could see the army of people on the course side-slipping the fresh snow out of the ruts, making the course faster. Then Lance charged off the starting pad and I couldn't see him through his vapor trail.

They'll be a little choppy this time, said my dad before he kissed me and told me to have fun.

When I crouched in the starting gate I noticed that the army of rut-cleaners was gone. The ruts were filling with snow and that would slow me down. Everybody was supposed to have similar snow conditions to level the field. The course was faster without snow in the ruts, so Lance had had a huge advantage on his run. A few gates lower I saw my dad waving his arms and yelling at one of the race officials. Then it was time to go.

The first rut took me by surprise. I had too much edge, too hard an angle, and my skis plowed into the snow. I jerked my knees up and out and was in the air, another tenth of a second lost. By the third turn I was back into my powder rhythm. As I moved into the flats the snow felt deeper and I did everything I could to glide instead of sink. The crowd roared as I came over the finish line and I knew I had lost.

I came to a stop and looked for him. Lance was somewhere inside the hustle-and-bustle and I checked the board. His combined score was two-tenths of a second faster than mine, meaning he had beaten me by a healthy seven-tenths on the second run. My dad skied up beside me and he whistled and his face was dimpled.

Done good Boy, he said.

I got the chills when they called my name to the podium. I stood to Lance's right and they hung the silver medallion over my neck. Afterward strangers shook my hand and my dad spoke to one of the coaches from Incline Village, a tall Swede wearing clogs.

He wants you on their team, Ollestad.

Really?

Yeah man. And guess who he's friends with.

I shrugged.

Ingmar Stenmark.

We were in the corner and I looked across the room and saw the Swede's head poking out from the crowd. Ingmar Stenmark was the greatest skier ever and my whole body inflated.

Tomorrow you're going to train with them, said my dad.

I was speechless.

Way to go, Ollestad.

Then the Heavenly Valley coach interrupted us.

Congratulations on taking second place, he said to me.

I nodded and my dad nodded.

You got pretty close. Lance had to take it up a notch on the second run, said the coach.

Yep, said my dad.

The coach waited as if expecting more from my dad.

I looked at my dad, come on, say it: Why didn't they slide the ruts for Norman?

We'll see you next month, was all my dad said.

The coach patted him on the shoulder and walked away. My dad never did mention their shenanigans and the following day I trained gates with the Incline ski team. Coach Yan gave me lots of attention, working with me on the hip-thrust weight change that made Ingmar so dominant. The other kids treated me with a respect I had never experienced and I was careful to be humble and not act like I was something special.

Sunday afternoon my dad and I left Tahoe and I had a new ski suit, padded sweater and all. When we passed the Heavenly Valley turnoff my dad said,

They've heard of Waterman now, Ollestad.

CHAPTER 23

S ANDRA'S WEIGHT PUSHED down on my shoulders as I cleated the thread of snow along the base of the rock wall. My whole body quivered with exhaustion. A tree limb appeared from the rock wall and I reached up and grabbed it. Sandra settled onto my other hand, nearly too small for her boot. Not clinging by fingernail, chin, pelvis and toe-tip was a huge relief. We did not speak, just resting.

It was time to move on. I told her we were almost there even though the chute did not seem to end, ever. The thread of snow would thin every few feet, making every inch without slipping a triumph. Having to hone my concentration blocked out the fact that we were moving too slowly and that night was only a couple hours away—that we were still, after all this time and effort, near the top of the mountain, thousands of feet above the meadow.

Locked into a pace, disciplining myself to be grateful for the progress, time passed, until I realized Sandra's boot was no longer touching my numb shoulder. I tilted my head to find her ankle. Not there. I looked up.

I was three or four feet below her. Both her arms reached high as if she were stretching out to sleep, even stranger because she was in a nearly vertical position.

Sandra. Get the stick down, I ordered. Push to your left.

She drew her knees under her stomach as if trying to stand up.

No, I yelled. Stay down.

From her knees she toppled over and plunged into the funnel, her limbs clambering as if trying to run uphill.

With my left hand I jabbed the withered stick into the snow. I reached for Sandra with my right hand. As I reached, her trajectory into the funnel shifted, routing her straight down. Her fingers struck my bicep and then her body plowed over me. I saw my hand grope her fancy boots—too far below me suddenly. She rocketed headfirst into the center of the funnel.

Norman! she screamed.

I was sliding too and I reached with my other arm and blindly grabbed a tree poking from the rocks.

My eyes never wavered from Sandra's boots, spewing thin vapors of ice. The fog swallowed her head, torso, and finally sucked away her feet. I heard her call my name one more time. It echoed and I heard it bouncing around in the fog.

You overreached. How could you do that? I snapped at myself in a harsh Nick-like tone. You failed to grab her and she was on top of you. Why were you lunging so far out?

One hand gripping the tree limb, I shrank under the judgments pounding inside my head. Bewildered, I gazed at my other arm dangling toward the funnel—a weak sapling, a worthless twig. I hung there, dwarfed by failure.

I have to make up for my mistake. Get to her quickly. I tried to move and slipped right away, grabbing the tree just in time. There was no rushing, no coercing the ice. I slowed down.

I followed her trail of blood smearing the center of the funnel. The thread of snow along the rock wall finally dissolved and I was forced into the funnel. On the left side where the ice was a millionth of a degree more supple, I moved fairly quickly, compared to before.

It's so much easier without the anchor. Now I have a chance to beat the night.

No, I scolded myself, smothering the image of Sandra weighted on my shoulders as I braced her perpetual fall.

Before the image had a chance to stir again I buried the terrible thought.

The ice curtain in the funnel demanded my every resource. I steered my whole mind onto the split-second decisions at the tip of my nose, drowning out my monumental mistake and the shameful relieved feeling that followed it. At one point the fog got so thick I ended up in the very center of the funnel where that millionth degree of harder ice tapped deeper into my single-minded concentration. It's too risky to try to get out of the center, I decided. More dangerous than just going with its flow.

I followed the trail of blood for a long time. I had determined that without an ice axe, or at least gloves, I would at some point lose traction—no tree or rock to save me this time. My hope was that I wouldn't go off a cliff or hit a tree on the way down, or collide with one of the trees at the bottom of the chute. But I was now hundreds of feet below the crash site and still alive, still conscious. It's just *ice-juice*, I told myself.

Slowly the funnel became shallower, less scooped out, and I made my way out of it onto the hard crust. I was back on the side of the chute we had started from, before getting sucked into the funnel. Thirsty, I rested for a few minutes and ate some snow. I noticed that both hands were raw to the bone across my first knuckles. There was no pain. It was too cold for pain. I ate snow until my thirst was quenched. Then I started down again.

I stayed close to the funnel, tracking the blood smear, which finally ended at a tree trunk—the first big tree since our descent began. There was no blood below it. I looked around for Sandra. I called out for her. No response. Only a rush of adrenaline urging me to find her, to make up for my mistake. It sickened me and I peered under wafts of fog, shuffling around, trying to shuck off the noxious shame.

Then I was inching downward again, trying to worry about the ice, not my mistake. I expected the pitch to ease—instead it seemed to dive away forever. I worried about that instead.

Just then streaks of red appeared in the snow. Sandra had hit that tree above me and kept falling. The shame registered again, but it lost out to the demands of the chute.

A splinter of malleable snow led me horizontally across the chute, away from the funnel, toward the other rocky border. Such firm ground for my hands and feet was impossible to resist. I followed it higher to a cluster of trees growing out of the rocky spine. I climbed up an embankment of snow onto a flat rock. I wrapped my arms around a trunk and worked myself onto my feet, numb to the bone. The trees reflected light and it was good to be out of the gray foam, and to feel a living thing—to hold it and sturdy myself with it.

The rocky spine bowed away into the fog and I stood on my tiptoes. Looking between two layers of gray—over the crest of fog and under the blanket of clouds—I caught a glimpse of the roof. It was closer, but I was still way above it. And now that I was farther down the chute the massive ridgeline was clearly too big to climb over. I would have to find a way through the gulch. What if there is no way through? My legs withered and I choked trying to get air into my lungs.

I imagined being trapped in the dark gulch, scratching at the rock walls trying to escape.

I glanced up, as if hoping to see the helicopter again. If they couldn't spot me when they were right over my head and the fog was thin, I thought, there was no chance under this lead ceiling. The peaks and valleys rambled for miles around here, gullies and dense forests. I was just a speck lost in it all.

Swinging astride the trunk I dropped my body over the spine of rock, hanging into the chute. I knew the snow was pulpy just below me so I let go of the tree and scaled down the embankment into the chute.

Move faster. It's getting late, I urged. Don't want to be up here in the dark. Then my foot hit a hard patch of crust and whoosh—I was flat on my belly and my sweater lifted to my chest and my belly rasped against the ice. I flopped onto my back, dug my heels, rebuffed by the impenetrable ice. Roaring now I flopped to my belly again and scratched at the ice.

Got to find soft snow!

I rolled to find it, snagged my knee on a crown of snow, and the abrupt halt pitched me into the air and I landed with my head leading the way. I thought of Sandra hitting that tree, and I heaved myself to one side, desperate for softer snow.

Several rotations. I was dizzy and slipping in and out of consciousness. The ice under my body felt as if it was thawing. Instinctively I dug in the heel of my palms, flattened my belly, and my hips and legs began to drag against the snow. It was a long, drawn-out deceleration. A blown tire limping to a stop. I lay there whipped and ragged.

CHAPTER 24

ON FRIDAY WE DROVE to Big Al's house. He was my dad's law partner and good friend. He was supposed to be all ready to go to Tahoe where I had a downhill race. My dad said that if I placed in the top three it would help my chances toward qualifying for the Southern Cal Championship race, only a month and a half away. My dad didn't knock and we found Al doing yoga in his living room wearing nothing but jockey underwear. He was tall like a basketball player and his feet were gigantic. His hair was reddish blond and his beard and eyebrows were the same color and bushy. My dad teased Al about being in a yogi trance and pretended to fight off a glare of light.

Your aura is blinding, said my dad.

Al ignored him, keeping his eyes closed, breathing through his nose methodically.

My dad grabbed some organic celery sticks with dirt still on them from the fridge. He dunked the celery into a jar of peanut butter and made me eat two whole sticks.

No time to stop for dinner, Ollestad.

Just after six the next morning we pulled into Uncle Joe's orange high-rise hotel. We quickly stowed our bags, changed into our ski gear and hit the road again.

Clear to the town of Truckee, Al did yoga breathing exercises. Gradually his exhalations became more forceful and louder. My dad told him to take it easy or he was going to be worn out before the first run.

We turned onto Highway 40 and Big Al pointed out the Donner Pass sign.

I was hungry but I just lost my appetite, said Al and my dad laughed.

What's so funny? I said.

Well, said Al. It's not really funny. Right around here is where the Donner Party got stuck in an early-season storm and half of them died.

What were they doing? I said.

Looking for a new frontier I guess. Problem was, they were ordinary people, not mountain people, and they got stuck in a big storm, said Al. The long and short of it is that some of them ended up having to eat their dead just to stay alive.

Gross, I said.

We climbed the winding highway and we all stared out the window at the mountains where those people had tried to survive.

I rode up with Coach Yan and we met the rest of the team at the top of the downhill course. We slipped it and spent a lot of time examining the S-turn. It dove over a pitch that fell away so that you couldn't see the slope beyond. There were nets to catch us if we lost control and flew toward the rocky ravines on each side.

The snow in the S-turn was especially hard, nearly ice, and I knew that this was where I could win the race. All those days skiing the wind-buffeted fifteen-foot lip of the Cornice in Mammoth, and having to carve the icy face of Mount Waterman, had prepared me well. Yan emphasized that we needed to come in high on the first part of the turn in order to go directly at the next two gates, setting up a straight shot into the final pitch and run-out.

Because of your light weight, Norman, you have to beat them here in the steeps, said Yan.

Yan was right, of course. Many times I had had the lead coming out of the steeps, only to lose the race to heavier kids who had the advantage on the flats.

My dad and Al hooted when they announced my number. Yan massaged my thighs and told me to keep the skis down and running after the S-turn. Don't lose any time in the flats, he reiterated. I felt loose and, most importantly, well attended to.

I attacked the upper course, taking an assertive line directly at the gates. I swooped in high on the S-turn and caught air over the fall-away pitch. I cursed myself for that but was thrilled by how much speed I had. I hit the long run-out and absorbed the humps and the ruffle sections where the skis tried to stammer. I plastered those fuckers to the snow.

I zipped over the dye and chattered to a stop. I was in third place, with Lance yet to race. I swore at the run-out and people turned their heads. I didn't care. How could I have gone so fast and not be the fastest? I couldn't go any better than that.

Yan arrived and told me I had the best time by three seconds coming out of the S-turn. I had lost over three seconds on the flats.

Why don't they make a fucking steep downhill course, I said.

Yan was taken aback by my foul mouth and my dad ushered me out of the finish area.

We rode up the chairlift and my dad was silent and he stared down at the snow passing like a highway beneath us. I felt bad about my outburst. I didn't say another word until after my second run.

Lance placed third and I placed fourth. In both runs I had been well ahead of the winner until I hit the flats. Yan said I was the best skier in the bunch and that success would come. We watched the awards ceremony and then it started to snow. Al had a hand-sized radio in his backpack and he tuned in the local weather. It was forecast to snow for two days and dump up to three feet. My dad called the office and he and Al conferred and by five that evening it was decided that we'd stay in Tahoe for a few extra days to ski some powder.

We skied good powder and the snow kept coming. My dad and Al decided to extend the trip further, pointing to the fact that I had a race in Yosemite the weekend upcoming and that there was no sense in Dad driving nine hours to Los Angeles, then back up here to northern California five days later.

For some reason my concentration was not at its best in Yosemite and I nearly hooked a couple gates on the first run. Once again I finished second (I think by one or two tenths). However the blow to my ego was mitigated when I realized that I had finally beaten Lance.

The next day he beat me in the giant slalom and I took second again. I was frustrated and thought I might not ever win. I was tortured by the idea that I was just not quite good enough. Was there something about me, a character flaw, that was holding me back?

Don't worry about winning, said my dad. It will come.

Why am I so small? I said.

You play the hand you're dealt, he said. Don't worry about trivial things like size and weight. Just put your head down and go for it.

I skulked past Al, who was watching us, quietly.

Shake it off, Ollestad, said Dad. All you can do now is focus on the next race.

We sought out one of Al's secret hot springs on the way home and my dad did backflips off a rock into the natural pool. I preferred cannonballs and Al was fine just soaking up the minerals that smelled like rotten eggs. We reminisced about skiing St. Anton when I was five and they spoke in code but I understood they were reliving their adventures with women.

Almost every weekend thereafter my dad and I drove out of town to the ski races. The San Bernardino Mountains were only two hours east of Los Angeles, but Mammoth was six hours north and Lake Tahoe was nine hours north. We'd roll back into town late Sunday night and the next morning my dad would drop me off at school, brushing his teeth in the car in front of all the other parents, which embarrassed me. I'd stay with my mom during the week and play with the neighborhood boys as much as possible. I finally acquiesced to my status as a semi-outsider—permanently orbiting on the fringe of their banter yet too athletic to be completely written off.

.   .   .

One day after school Nick drove me in his station wagon to the University of Southern California campus. On our way to the football field to watch the Trojans practice he pointed out the halls where, he said, kids not much older than I studied as hard as they could so that they could get the good jobs and make lots of money and live the way they wanted. He added that there were fun parties and *beautiful dames* too.

He was a diehard USC fan and I asked him if he had gone there.

No. But all my friends did, he said. I hung around here so much everybody thought I did.

Learning that Nick did not go to college gave his message a special resonance. He wasn't trying to make me be like him. Sort of the opposite, in fact. I wondered why Nick drove me all the way down here to show me this. He was actually kinda cool when he didn't drink, I thought.

Education was the theme that week. After my hockey game on Friday night my dad told me that if I stuck with hockey I might be able to earn a scholarship to Harvard or Yale. I asked him why he didn't go there.

Well I couldn't afford it, he said. And I didn't play hockey or ski race. Plus UCLA was right here and a pretty good school.

So why don't I just go to UCLA too?

You can. But Harvard is better.

We were back in Lake Tahoe, at Squaw Valley. It was a big race—the top three finishers overall, from J3 to J5, would qualify to try out for the Junior Olympic Team, and certainly qualify for the Southern Cal Championship race.

At breakfast that first morning I talked freely with my new teammates, describing powder skiing with my dad, hockey triumphs, surfing Mexico, cannonballs at a secret hot springs, and they responded with wide-eyed grins and asked me lots of questions, the antithesis of those blank faces back home. Feeling valued got me so excited that I talked through the entire breakfast and couldn't wait for lunch.

The snow was hard and Yan said the course was tight like the way they set them in Europe. It was on the same hill as the 1960 Olympic slalom course and my dad called Al and told him. We slid the course twice and the pitch was unrelenting, no breather sections, with two flushes in steep hangs.

On the first run I stayed high and took it easy, positioning myself fifth overall, which gave me confidence. On the second run I let the ruts sling me from turn to turn and I thrust my hips for extra bursts of speed. For the entire run I was on the verge of out of control.

I won my division and finished third overall and for the rest of the weekend my dad called me Ingmar Ollestad.

During the car ride home I voiced my hopes and dreams.

I think I can win the So Cal Championship next weekend and make the Junior Olympic Team, I said.

Absolutely, said my dad.

CHAPTER 25

I'M BREATHING HARD. I must be alive. You're lucky you didn't hit a tree on that tumble.

My stomach burned and my head tingled. Translucent diamonds waltzed amid the falling snow. Everything whirled and I thought about going to sleep. This is just a nightmare. I'll wake from the dream and we'll be landing in Big Bear. There was my dad carrying me off the plane.

Gradually my eyes found focus. The chute had widened. The rock borders on each side had melted into the slope. I figured I must be near the wooded section.

I sat up. It was not as steep. My whole body decompressed. But that gave way to a rush of images—Dad's curly hair, his head on his knees, arms dangling, fading to an ice sculpture slipping away into a casket of mist.

I tried to shake it off. My mind reeled, desperate to escape the fact that my dad was actually dead. I needed blue sky. A place to ascend to that was not this gray universe where death and pain and cold ruled. But all I could see was ashen cloud pressing down from all sides. Even so I tried to imagine my life thriving beyond this sludge. Nothing. I saw myself as a flame tussling in a draft alone in a barren world. I missed Sandra's mumbo-jumbo.

I just sat there staring at the gateway to what I knew was the wooded section beyond the fog. My mind refused to initiate anything, too absorbed in my dire circumstances. I can't. I can't do this anymore, echoed in my head.

But my body moved. As if my muscle memory heard my dad's voice, *Go for it Boy Wonder. You can do it.* I stood up.

I wandered across the chute to a tree and broke the ends off a couple limbs. Paring away the needles released their familiar scent and it gave me a boost, setting my mind into motion. An idea blipped. I dropped to my butt and began sliding downward, a stick in each hand to control my speed and turn around trees or crags of rock.

The spine of rocks to my left gathered back into a formidable border and this last few yards of the chute fed into a rivulet-like channel that ran along the base of the border. I went with the flow and saw patches of blood in the rivulet. My quickened pace and the idea that I was now beating the night charged me. At this speed I had a chance, I kept telling myself.

The border of rock blunted and I came around a small cliff face. Sandra's body lay in my path. She was on her back. Her boot tips pointed into the air. Her hair flowed out from her head, dark against the white snow. I was afraid to call her name, afraid she wouldn't move.

She was in a wooded enclave of tall spruces. Just above her was my airplane seat, leaning against a tree. I stood and my feet plunged. I couldn't move. The snow clung to my thighs like quicksand. Every strand of muscle in my legs burned as I lurched to unplug my drenched sneakers from the snow. I staggered toward Sandra, calling her name. But she didn't answer.

Her eyes were wide open. Skin purple. I stood over her and she stared right at me. I kneeled and my legs trembled with fatigue. I shook her. I spoke to her.

Are you there? Sandra. Sandra. Your eyes are open.

I got right down in her face. You just slipped, I said. You'll be all right. Let's go!

She stared into the leaden gray and her body was stiff like a mannequin. She was dead. A stark fact, confused by her intense gaze.

The mistake, my overreach in the chute, piled on my shoulders and I needed to hide from it. I stamped and bucked like an animal then shrank down into what felt like a thicker skin. Huddled, my body was sapped of power, ravaged by all the death, the bleakness ahead, and I had no strength left for shame, for anything.

I let precious time pass, hunkered there. Then a growl rumbled in my chest and sent up a burst of energy. I rose onto my knees and hands, swinging my head upward to stand. I broke twigs from the spruce limbs, spending more precious time covering her body and face, leaving two openings for her eyes.

I have to go, I said.

CHAPTER 26

WE LEFT TOPANGA Sunday morning at 5:00 a.m., headed for the championship race. My dad and I wore Levis and T-shirts, and Sandra had on a parka. I cramped in the back of the Porsche on top of my hockey bag with my sticks on the floor—ready for my game that night after the ski race. My dad and I sang country songs all the way to Big Bear while Sandra slept on her pillow against the passenger window.

It was a clear day. The sun came up right over the Snow Summit ski resort, edging a pink halo behind the yellowish rotting snow. I had breakfast with the Mountain High ski team and realized during breakfast that I was racing for Mountain High today. When I asked my dad why, he said that in order to race in the Southern California Championships I had to be on a Southern California team, not the Incline team—even though I was from farther south than anyone else racing. My dad had arranged all this and in his typical fashion slid me into a whole new world as if it were just a minor detail. Without a fuss, without resentment, I reframed the situation, like Dad always seemed to do. Just a new name, the rest is the same: same gear, same mountain, same skis, same race. Looking at it like that was sure a lot easier than fighting it. At the end of breakfast Dad presented me with a fancy new Spyder race sweater to complete the transformation.

The snow had turned to solid ice over the last few days. By noon it would soften and my dad hoped they got the race going right away so that my second run wouldn't be in the slush. The course was set much like Squaw Valley—steep and tight.

At 9:30 I took my first run. My line was too aggressive, a bit cocky, and I had to gouge the ice to make up for my poor angles. Still I was tied for first place with Lance, who was racing for Big Bear.

When the girls took their first run the sun was high and the snow was getting soft. Dad said there was a fast-moving shot of moisture coming in off the ocean, which was only eighty miles away. And by the time the girls were done I felt spindles of cool air wafting over the ridges and saw wispy clouds.

Come on baby, said my dad up at the clouds. Keep it cool for us.

After lunch ruffled blankets of cumulus striped the sky and the cool breeze was steady, keeping the snow hard enough to be to my advantage.

Let it all hang out, Ollestad, said my dad.

Come in high. Nice smooth turns, Norman, said the Mountain High coach.

Racer ready, called the starter, who then began the countdown. I adjusted my goggles under the rim of my helmet. A deluge hit my bladder and I pinched my thighs together, catching it in time. I cocked my wrists, guiding my pole tips over the wand and into the holes, arms stretched forward like Superman in flight.

Two . . . one . . . Go! said the starter.

My chest shot out between my hands and I drove my poles downward as my heels kicked back, rocking me onto my toes. My whole body launched off the pad before my boots tripped the wand. I came in high on the first gate. I brushed the gate and sliced up under it setting up my next turn. As the hill got steeper the ruts got deeper. My skis bent, uncoiling as I came out of the pockets, flinging me into the air. So I pulled my knees in on the next turn and felt my skis suck up the rut. One more gate to go, then the flush. I was well ahead of the turns and charged into the flush. Five quick edge changes—five quick turns through this tight section of gates. Slithering out of the flush the next rut bent 90 degrees, and when I hit it my kneecaps rammed my chin. Stars and the taste of blood. I was late into the next turn. Half blind, I chiseled my edges into the ice and abruptly released them, bouncing off the rut floor and into the air, losing some time in the process. When my skis touched down I set them on the proper line and spit out the blood before compressing into the next rut. Spit, compress, pivot the weight. Another jagged trough. Delicate edge work. Light as a cat. I found my way back into a good rhythm.

When I came through the finish line I choked on the blood. I coughed it up and spit onto the snow. My dad skied beside me. I looked up and his insatiable grin said it all.

Am I in first? I said to make sure.

Yep. Two more racers, he said. You okay?

I nodded. Lance's coming now, I said, pointing up the hill.

He whizzed through the flush and ka-banged into that gorge of a rut and was thrown back onto the tails of his skis—never regaining control all the way to the finish line. My dad and I swung around to the board. My combined time was faster.

The next racer hit the first rut on the top and I saw him flip over. D.Q.

My dad nodded. Looked down at me. His face was placid. His smile was gentle.

You won, Ollestad.

I raised my arms and spit more blood. We stared at each other. I saw him so clearly. The cranium shelf rising off his forehead bumpy and uneven, the cluster of diamonds in the blue of his eyes fragile cracked windows, and I saw someone younger and full of grand ambitions and I thought about how he had wanted to be a professional baseball player. He looked at me as if into a mirror, studying me, like I was holding something that he admired, even desired.

Way to kick ass, he said.

Thanks, I said.

The Mountain High coach skated over and patted me on the butt.

Good skiing, he said.

He looked at me intensely too. It felt like there was a small fire in my cupped hands and everybody wanted to savor its heat.

Finally, I said.

CHAPTER 27

I *TURNED AWAY FROM* Sandra's body, shielded by twigs, and surveyed the landscape. From the crash site I had mapped out this elliptical apron and the tight gulch below it. I had to control my descent down the apron and, hopefully, forge that gulch, then I would find the meadow and, below somewhere in the woods, the road that would lead me to shelter.

As far as I could see the apron was perfect for my energy-saving technique of sliding on my butt. Off I went. After a few minutes I realized that I was turning around markings in the snow—rock tips, bumps, animal tracks, anything—and that I was whooping as if it was a slalom course. This playful whim struck me as careless so I stopped whooping, went straight, only turning to control my speed.

Nearly a thousand feet later the slope tapered into the gulch and the sides of the gulch rose like two tidal waves of rock about to slam together. I was deep in its heart. The pitch got steeper and I alternated between skimming on my ass and flopping onto my stomach to cleat the snow with my sticks.

As I descended, the terrain mutated into uneven rock mixed with snow, and the pitch tilted close to 35 degrees. It was too dangerous now. I had to stay on my belly.

Slowing down gave the gathering night a chance to over-take me. Each methodical step and fingerhold over the broken ground became a chore. Soon both sides pinched so tight I was forced toward the creek bed. I had sensed it down there in the crevice and wanted to avoid it at all cost. Getting wet would surely slow me down. Might give me hypothermia.

I noticed shrubs squeezing from the rock and decided it was worth taxing my strength to get to them. I used cracks in the rock, wedging my frozen fingers into them to traverse the dicey overhang above the creek. I got hold of the shrubs and lowered myself as close to the creek's edge as possible. I was short by about two feet.

I eyed the transparent layer of ice coating the slurry of water that flashed beneath like schools of silver fish. Recalling how my dad almost froze when he had gotten wet during one of our backcountry powder adventures, I knew I had to stick the landing. Fall sideways, not backward, if you lose balance, I told myself.

Lowering my body, my hands slithered down the vine and I dropped. My feet plunged into the snow and I teetered back-ward. I forced myself to one side, landing on my hip, avoiding the creek. The buried foot did not release and I felt my knee tweak. I got up on my hands to relieve my knee. I pulled my feet out and started moving. The knee hurt but it worked.

The wall on this side was too vertical, and the bench of snow next to the creek was too narrow. So I jumped the four-foot-wide creek. The creek bench was only a foot wider on this side and I had to descend on my hip, with my back to the creek, facing the gulch wall. Using nubs in the gulch wall to control my speed I slid down on my hip—an unproven technique. A mistake here would be disastrous. Don't slip off this bench of snow, I warned. You'll freeze and that'll be the end.

I maneuvered my body into a chain of contortions, spidering the bench of snow between the gulch wall and the creek. A couple hundred feet lower I had staked out a landing site—a rock surface shaped like a bowl with no water in it. I hoped that either to the right or left of it there would be a needle hole through the bulwark of rock.

The tedium made my eyes dry and itchy, and I started to blink incessantly. Later I stopped in a good place and shut my eyes for a few minutes. Then I opened them to assess my progress. Not even halfway to that bowl-shaped rock, still over a hundred feet below.

I went back to the tedium of inch-by-inch, crag-by-crag, nail-by-nail progress. The minute details at my nose were my entire universe.

By the time I made it to the rock bowl it was noticeably darker. I scrutinized the clouds hoping they were the culprit. But they had dissipated in the gulch and hovered way up the sidewalls. Overcome with dread that ate away at my resolve, I succumbed to the numbness and exhaustion and hunger gnawing to be recognized. It hit me all at once and I plunked down onto the cold rock, whacking my chin against my knee. Just like when I rammed that gorge of a rut, I thought. If only I had wiped out during the race then I wouldn't have won that stupid trophy, and we wouldn't have gotten on the plane. This stopped my mind in its tracks and I rested down, as if to sleep.

I thought about my dad not allowing me to eat junk food. One particular time at my Pop Warner football team banquet, which Nick took me to, the coach tore open boxes of Snickers and Hershey and Three Musketeers bars and we all raced toward the feast. I had grabbed my favorite—a Three Musketeers—when my dad appeared out of nowhere. No way, Ollestad, he said. I cursed him and he told me he would always be there, even when I was sixteen on a date with a girl about to open a beer he would pop out from the backseat and say, Ah-ha!

Again my body reacted when my mind was too weary and I lifted up off the cold rock. I searched for the best way to proceed.

The gulch bent 90 degrees, leading toward a crack into a wider gully or canyon. But the rock floor just ended, a cliff for sure I thought. The other sides of the rock bowl climbed upward and integrated back into the massive ridgeline. I had to go wherever the gulch took me.

On all fours I crabbed backward, following the rock floor. Below me the rock was shiny with patches of ice and I had no reason to believe there would be anything to hold on to once I went over the edge.

As I approached the edge I lay on my belly. Feet first, I wiggled over the brim. It was a dry waterfall, except to my far right where a vein of water poured down the face. The throat of the waterfall was composed of icy rock blisters stacked vertically. At least in the chute I had a chance of avoiding a collision if I slipped, but here the waterfall emptied into slabs of big and pointed shale about fifty feet below me.

There was no decision-making process. I had to go. So I went. Using the curved sidewall and whatever cracks I could find along the face to leverage between, I spread my limbs horizontally. I wormed my way down the face crease by crease, my numb fingertips and toe tips inexplicably culling the flaky holds and discovering tiny leverage points.

Then I dropped off the last icy rock onto the body-size chips of shale. I paused for a moment. The fog had lifted into the soupy clouds, I could see for hundreds of feet, and I was finally off the steeps. But I was running out of daylight. I took a couple breaths and labored forward. The meadow must be close.

CHAPTER 28

M Y DAD HUSTLED ME to the Snow Summit lodge and we put all our ski stuff in a locker. Then we went to the bar to get Sandra.

When do I get the trophy? I said.

The ceremony's tomorrow, President's Day, he said.

But if I just get it now then we won't have to come back, I said.

That's not how they're doing it, he said. Plus you can train with the team tomorrow.

We entered the bar and Sandra was pretty buzzed. She wanted to stay the night.

Little Norman's got a hockey game, said my dad.

Well fuck, Norm, she said. Everybody stop. Just stop what you're doing, she announced to the bar. This little blond boy has a hockey game so the world has to stop.

We're leaving so come on, said my dad.

He turned and I followed him out the door. It was warm again and the clouds were gone. Looking over a far ridge, Dad thanked the storm for sending the cool air.

I guess we just caught the edge of it, he added.

Trailing behind us, Sandra cursed and bitched all the way to the Porsche.

There's no fucking relaxing, she said. Go here. Go there. Go go go GO!

My dad reversed out of the parking spot, put the car in first gear and gripped the steering wheel with both hands.

I'm glad we're taking a fucking plane tomorrow, she said.

Me too, I said.

We'll be able to see your championship run from the air, he said.

Cool.

Better take a catnap, he said. Big game tonight.

Okay, I said.

I curled up against the back window.

CHAPTER 29

THE GIANT SHALE moated by snow proved more grueling than I had anticipated. This terrain wasn't nearly as steep and there was no ice or cliffs, but the gummy snow clutched my sneakers and I had to stand instead of slide, taxing my last reserves of strength. I was forced to bend and twist over the sharp uneven shapes, constantly losing my footing, entrenched again and again—an unpleasant reminder of my utter weariness and hunger. My stomach seemed to chew on itself.

Soon I had nothing left. I had no energy for a reaction, not even despair. I literally stumbled onto a tuft of snow that cropped up like a miracle. The giant shale seemed to melt away into this alluvial fan of snow like a turbulent stream feeding into glassy, slow water. I looked up, maybe for the first time in half an hour.

Two hundred yards downslope glimmered a pure white plate of snow—the meadow. It was partially eclipsed by intermittent hedges of buckthorn bush poking from the snow. I imagined charging for the meadow but sensed that the fan of snow ahead was unstable—beneath it the buckthorn bush, crushed like mattress springs, was a trap. Sprouting out here and there, the bush looked like a decaying maze. I rehearsed weaving through it and onto the meadow. My eyes tracked the surface, sniffing out potential danger points. Right in front of me was a deceivingly firm snowdrift—a coil of buckthorn that would break underfoot. I identified a few more areas to avoid, then stood numb and fatigued, shivering from my bones outward. It was as if my cartilage and my ligaments had dried out and I wondered if I was going to break apart like brittle wood.

I leaned toward the meadow, drawn to it, a dehydrated animal spotting a water hole. My first step was Frankenstein-like. I heaved one leg out of the snow and lurched forward. My head was light as if there were no brain inside my skull. I wavered, unable to balance in the variable crust that changed to heavy cement and back to crust from one step to the next. I had to stop. Breathe. Find my balance.

Again I lurched forward. This time I let my momentum carry me downhill. When the snow turned soft underfoot I used my stomach to suck up my weight like skiing breakable crust or Sierra Cement with my dad.

As I hobbled down the fan of snow, my mind flickered with muddled images that burned under a Mexican sun. No emotion, just faint smeared orange and yellow colors—Me, Grandpa, Dad, swimming in an ocean as warm as a bathtub.

My eyes were closed when the crust broke wide open. I danced my weight to my other foot and it caved too. I jiggered laterally and my magic ran out. I plummeted, knifing deep into the buck-thorn. When I settled I was nearly entombed, only my head and one hand branching out of the snow.

I spit to clear snow from my mouth. I reached up with my free arm and the surface collapsed into my hole. My sneakers checked against the tangle of vines and I dropped a few inches deeper.

It's like a tree well, I thought. I pictured my dad wedging his feet and arms against the sides and working his way up and out. I can do the same.

The vines gave way the instant I loaded against them. I willed my body upward and the limbs bent, worthless.

Some serrated leaves were still attached to the vine and when I moved again my ski pants and sweater pulled against the whole gnarl, quaking the snow around me.

Nothing was working, and nothing seemed like it would work. I was at the end of my tether. There was a flare of anger and frustration, abruptly smothered out, as if all the circuits in my brain were fizzling, and I shut down.

CHAPTER 30

M Y DAD WAS in the bleachers at the beginning of the second period like he promised. He had taken Sandra home because she had refused to sit in the cold ice rink. Right off the drop I ended up with the puck and split the defense with a burst of speed up the middle. There was no one to pass it to and the goalie charged out of his crease and kept coming so I stick-handled left, tucked the puck in and reversed direction. The goalie's body was going the wrong way and I slid the puck under his outstretched glove.

Nice move, Ollestad, my dad called from the bleachers.

My teammates gave me high fives and the coach kept me on the ice. By the end of the second period I had an assist to go along with my goal.

After the game some of the kids on the other team complimented my play and I went to bed that night feeling like I was on a good roll. I really am all those things Dad keeps saying I am. Good enough to beat the bigger, stronger kids. Tougher than tiger shit—maybe even tiger piss. And tomorrow I will have a championship trophy to prove it.

CHAPTER 31

I WAS PHYSICALLY AND mentally parched, stuck in a hole, tangled in indomitable vines and semi-unconscious. Like something pushing through a thick jungle, I became aware of myself again. A vague idea rustled me—a few feet away was something to grab, a hedge. I began to see my surroundings again—the backside of the massive ridgeline was a crown of rock jutting forward like a ragged ship prow. I'm close, close to the meadow, I reminded myself. I could use my fingernails, lunge—I ran through strategies. In spite of these whispered calls to action I didn't actually move.

I heard a noise overhead. I looked up and saw a big airplane belly. The fog had completely given way to a heavy graphite-colored sky. The plane banked and I used my free hand to wave at it. I kept my eyes glued to it.

Miraculously it circled around. I waved and watched it come back over the meadow again. I waved and yelled. They can see me. I'm saved. Then it sailed over the ridge. They saw me. That's why they circled.

I waited for a long time and the plane did not come back and no one came to save me or called out for me. The wind sounded like voices and I yelled, but only the wind answered.

The graphite sky was edged in black—night was creeping in, maybe an hour away. I felt depleted again, woozy, bleary-eyed. I figured that my struggle was over and that I was going to die.

CHAPTER 32

AD WOKE ME at 5:30 in the morning. Sandra was in the living room warming her hands over the potbelly stove. It took me a moment to remember why we were all up so early—the plane ride back to Big Bear.

As I laced up my Vans I noticed a couple of new photographs on the judge's desk that was given to my dad by a penniless client as payment for keeping his son out of jail. Next to the old black-and-white photo of me harnessed to my dad's back as he surfed a two-footer off the point was a color photo of Dad, Grandpa, and me swimming that day we arrived in Vallarta, our three heads poking out of the water like sea lions. Beside that was another one of Dad and me skiing in St. Anton, Austria—boot-deep powder—in which I'm leading the way with my *deadly snow-plow that could cut through anything,* as my dad liked to say.

Who took the picture of us skiing in St. Anton? I said.

He came out of the bathroom naked, brushing his teeth.

I had a professional do it. Pretty nifty, huh?

It's great. We're both shredding.

Sandra walked over.

I wonder how big the trophy's going to be, she said.

Should be pretty big. Right? I said.

Who cares about a *trophy*, said my dad. You know you won—that's all that matters.

CHAPTER 33

I *WAS TRAPPED, WORN OUT* and frozen. Night moved down on me like a mass of crows swooping in from all sides of the sky. I closed my eyes against them—wanting to fall asleep before they ate me.

Something like a jiggle wormed its way inside me. Something bigger, from the core of the earth, was counting out time. A drop of dew jiggling on a leaf, that faint.

I sensed the wind whistling through the gullies and heard it cut across the snow. Ice peppered my face. It dawned on me that I was still stuck and still cold and therefore still alive. I watched another gust peel off a skin of snow like grains of sandpaper ripping free. It made me think of a barren graveyard in a ghost town. I conjured my dad and me in Bodie, the cool dusk chasing us to the car, Dad saying the temperature had dipped from three-king cold to four-king cold, giving me license to say, That's four-king A right.

I looked at the buckthorn rising out of the snow several

yards away. I kicked at the buckthorn entwined with my legs and torso under the snow. No way to get to that first hedge.

Even so I stretched one arm toward the first hedge and my body floated in that direction. The snow caved and I circled my weight in ten different directions at once—a slow-motion dog paddle, treading water in the sea of vines. Intuitively my armpit, some ribs and a hip found a place to caress the vines and I delicately leaned, settling.

Like a gymnast swinging his legs over the horse, I lifted onto a ball of vines that buoyed against my hip. My feet then pushed off and I rose out of the hole. I was careful not to let my upper body reach too far across the snow and risk plunging headfirst into the next quadrant of mesh.

Then the vines collapsed. I pitched my hip under me and drove my legs downward, spreading all limbs, catching like a thorny lobe in dog hair.

Again I ventured one arm out. The snow felt solid before me. I spread my legs out in the mesh, dispersing the load. Under my forearm the crust was firm. I slithered chin, chest, then stomach onto this atoll. It cracked and I rolled onto my back. As the pane shattered I wheeled my feet and drove them down, ensuring they went first with the rupturing snow into the gnarl below. Sprawling wide again to ensnare the buckthorn, my head bobbled out of the hovel. There was the hedge. A leap away.

I lunged at it. Unfortunately I had no leverage and ended up sinking deeper into my pit. I tried again. Broadening my load this time, I uncoiled gracefully as I stretched one arm out. I eased over the lip of the pit. My fingers tickled the underside of the hedge. A little wiggle and my torso followed my arm out of the hole. I skated for an instant across the crust, then grabbed a throng of vines. My lame dexterity was salvaged by the tight weave of vines clasping me as much as I clasped them.

When the snow broke at my waist both hands snapped off the bush and I barely shot my arm up in time to snag the hedge with one hand. My legs fell and lodged in the netting below. Then I got my other hand clutched to the hedge and kicked away the nagging spurs. I lifted my body up into the hedge and snaked my legs deep into its gnarl. I hung to the face of the hedge and it bowed toward the snarling chasm. There was no fucking way I was letting go.

Then I understood that I could drop my legs and swivel from hand to hand along the face of the hedge. I moved, my numb feet tottering like dead stumps over the crust. I traversed the hedge as if swinging from rings in a playground. I made it to the end of the hedge. There was a three- or four-foot gap to the next spate growing out of the snow. I peered through the bush but could not locate the meadow. I knew it was close though.

I reached out with my leg and felt that the snow beneath was firm enough for me to rest some of my weight on it. I gathered my bearing and lowered onto my stomach, spreading my weight. The ground felt solid so I shimmied across the crust and grabbed the next hedge. This allowed me to stand again because I had the hedge to hold onto.

I walked on top of the snow and held on to the hedge so as not to put too much weight on the tenuous crust. The buckthorn spates grew closer and closer together as I moved downslope. I scurried from one to the other and only fell through a couple times. It was easy to pull myself out with the hedge right there. Then I saw the meadow. My eyes fixed on the oasis, nothing else.

CHAPTER 34

A GUARD LET US through the draw gate into Santa Monica Airport. It was desolate. The sky was gray and dull. We parked behind a building underneath the control tower. We walked in. My dad knocked on a door and a man a few years younger than he emerged. His name was Rob Arnold. His sandy blond hair was cut just below his ears and it was combed down neatly, reminding me of those straitlaced guys who came from the city to surf Topanga. He was our pilot. We were all set to go.

CHAPTER 35

WHEN I CAME to the edge of the meadow the snow had compressed the buckthorn, making a four- or five-foot lip on this side of the meadow. I slid over the lip and into the foamy oasis. Wading through the soft snow, moving upright across even ground, shocked me—it broke the spell that had channeled every bit of energy, mental and physical, into one singular focus. I stopped moving. I wanted to give up. Quit. Sit down and refuse to do this. All that I had witnessed over the last eight hours suddenly made me violently angry.

I stood there enraged. The spiking fury kept me from sitting down on the cushioned ground. The anger was hot. For the first time since the crash I didn't feel cold. My fingers and feet were numb but my face and torso and thighs were actually warm.

Now all that mattered was not getting cold again—and in a flash I was back under the spell that drove me down the mountain and wrenched me out of those buckthorn vines like a wolf smelling fresh meat ahead.

I trudged across the meadow. I searched for an opening in the tight weave of buckthorn and oak trees on the downhill side. I walked the perimeter. The forest was too dense. There seemed no way to get to that road I had spotted from up high. How the hell do you get out of this place?

I saw something but the light was dappled. I ducked under the canopy and kneeled. It was a boot print. Pocking the snow with little squares. Like my dad's boots. He was still up there getting battered by the blizzard. My knee felt too heavy to lift off the ground, as if squashed by something. His slumped body that wouldn't flinch when I shook him blurred my thoughts. I was down here and he was way up there. He would have carried me down with him, no doubt in my mind.

I forced myself to study the snow—*bear down and grind it out*. The boot prints were fresh. There were more.

Narrowing my aim on the boot prints seemed to tuck me back into my wolfish pelt—more natural to me now than my eleven-year-old-boy skin.

The terrain came into sharp focus. I lifted my knee and crawled forward following the prints down the hillside. A chaotic, circuitous route. Kids playing, I guessed. And there's a big one. An adult. Their dad. I was on my feet, staggering over their trail. It lured me left and right, tunneling me under the cluster of bush, plants and oak limbs. Each square notch in the snow reached into my gut, guiding me forward. The prints would lead to that road.

I heard something. A voice.

CHAPTER 36

*P*ILOT ROB LED us across the tarmac toward one of several four-seater Cessna airplanes lined up in a row. My dad looked up at the flat gray sky.

Do you think the weather's okay to fly in? he asked Rob.

Yeah. Just a couple clouds, said Rob. We'll stay below them probably. Should be a smooth flight.

My dad glanced at the sky one more time.

All right, he said.

CHAPTER 37

THE WIND HAD tricked me before, so I ignored the voice. The boot tracks made a circle and I followed it around until I realized I was backtracking. Ripples of panic set off my adrenaline and my body jittered. It was hard to concentrate. I needed to delineate the chaos of prints before me but my head was clouded by the surging adrenaline.

Hello! Anybody there! echoed in the canyon.

I blinked. The voice seemed to come from everywhere. I riveted my eyes to those boot prints, not wanting them to somehow disappear—they were real but the voice might not be. I yelled back.

Help! Help me!

Hello! someone called back, and it didn't sound like the wind.

Help! I responded.

Keep yelling, said a boy. I'll follow your voice.

I kept yelling and I ran down the hillside, toward my best

estimation of where the voice was coming from. I darted around the small oaks like racing poles. I came out into milky light at the dirt road.

Holy shit. I made it.

As I staggered down the road I called out for the voice.

I heard it coming from just around the bend. Suddenly a dog appeared. Skinny. Brown. Then a teenage boy, wearing a jacket over a Pendleton flannel. He froze in his tracks. I walked toward him.

Are you from the crash? he said.

It was weird that he knew, I thought. Yes, I said.

Is there anybody else up there?

Yes. My dad and his girlfriend Sandra. The pilot's dead.

What about your dad?

Before I could stop it, it spilled out of me.

Dead or just knocked out, I said. I shook him but he didn't wake up.

The teenager stared at me. His stunned expression and my saying *dead* out loud unleashed the bleakness of it all—my dad is gone forever. He will never again wake me for hockey practice, never again lure me into a wave, never again point out the beauty in some storm. Pain attacked my bones, brittle and cold and easy to crush. An unbearable weight mounted on my back and my legs and feet trembled and I couldn't look at the teenager's sad face anymore. He was living proof that it was all real, that Dad was dead.

I looked at the ground and my spine strained to keep me from collapsing.

Should I carry you? he said.

No I'm fine, I said.

He picked me up anyway and I didn't resist. He laid me across his outstretched arms. They felt like knives and the pain shot through my body and spiked through my head and it hurt so bad that I contorted—mind and body buckling into a pretzel.

As he carried me down the road I stared back at the mountain. Although it was smothered in boils of cloud, I knew vividly what was inside that storm, and for an instant the whole arc of my life was clear to me: Dad coaxing me past boundaries of comfort, day after day, molding me into his little masterpiece, even Nick's vile fingers of doubt that I was left to fight alone, it was all completely transformed. Every misadventure, every struggle, everything that had pissed me off and made me curse Dad sometimes, rippled together, one scene tripping the next, the pieces speeding forward like falling dominoes into a streak.

I glared at the storm as it feasted on the mountain, hammering on my dad still trapped in there. It did not get me. And I knew—I knew that what he had put me through saved my life.

In the charcoal gray dusk the teenager, who said his name was Glenn Farmer, carried me toward a sawmill that was next to a ranch house. A tall blond woman was standing outside the sawmill watching us approach. She moved into the middle of the road and Glenn carried me right to her. She winced at my black-and-blue eyes, blood-encrusted lacerations, and raw knuckles, but just for an instant, then her heavily hooded eyelids relaxed, softening her gaze.

Are you from the plane crash? she said.

I was startled that she knew too. I nodded.

My name's Patricia Chapman, she said. You're safe now.

She called into the sawmill. A man in overalls came out. This was her husband Bob. I told him what had happened and where to find Sandra and my dad.

Then Patricia walked me to her house. She tugged the heavy

block of wood open and ushered me inside. An old Native American rug cushioned my feet. I saw two low-slung rocking chairs facing a potbelly stove like the one in my dad's house. I could feel the heat defrosting my skin all the way from the doorway.

Sit down, she said.

The chair was something amazing, the way it cradled me and let me rest. I reached my hands and feet toward the embers. She asked me if I wanted hot chocolate.

Yes please.

Patricia said she was a mom and that her two sons were playing down at the far end of the road. I stared into the pink-red glow throbbing beyond the open door of the potbelly stove. I wondered if they had bikes or skateboards.

A few minutes later Patricia handed me a mug of hot chocolate. She sat in the other rocking chair and we both leaned forward. My feet tingled and needles shot up my ankles and shins. The hot cocoa and the radiating stove thawed my hands.

There was a crippling pain in my right hand and I noticed that it was swollen so I switched the mug to the other hand.

Patricia asked me if there was anything else I wanted.

No. Just to get warm.

She was relaxed and patient. We sat quietly, staring at the fire. I felt myself adapting to the calm and warmth of the room. My first rest in more than nine hours.

After I finished my hot chocolate she said she thought she had better call somebody and let them know I was okay. I nodded.

Patricia called the Mount Baldy fire station from the other room and came back and told me they would meet us at the gate by the highway. I got up and took her hand and she led me out the door.

We walked under the last whisper of light down a path through pools of snow and around big reddish-brown tree trunks. Patricia told me the footprints I had spotted leading down from the meadow were hers and her sons'. I asked her why she went there.

Just had a feeling, she said.

I thought about us both being drawn to the meadow, about the helicopter not being able to help me, about how only she helped me—her footprints were like a yellow brick road.

At a wooden gate by the main road I saw a fire truck, an ambulance and a couple unmarked cars. Guys in suits stood in front of the cars. They approached as a group while a paramedic looked me over. When he was done one of the men wearing a suit stepped forward. Detective So-and-So. He was taking me to the Ontario hospital. I waved good-bye to Patricia.

On the way down the winding road the detective asked me questions about the crash. Who was flying? Was I sure it was not my dad? Did I notice anybody suspicious when I boarded the plane? Did the pilot say anything before we hit the mountain? Was something wrong with the plane? I told him what I knew, and twenty minutes later we arrived at the hospital.

CHAPTER 38

I WAS LYING ON my back looking into a lamp. The faces of a nurse and doctor stared down at me while they stitched up my chin. The doctor sutured it from the inside, going through my mouth, then from the outside. He then worked on the punctures in my cheeks.

You're doin' great, said the doctor. When I'm done, is there anything you want to eat or drink?

I hadn't eaten in more than twelve hours. My stomach grumbled.

Yeah. A chocolate milkshake, I said.

I sort of held my breath after I said it, half expecting my dad's voice to boom out, No way, Ollestad. How about a turkey sandwich on wheat?

No one objected. And the doctor called out to someone to fix up a chocolate milkshake right away.

When he was finished stitching my face I sat up and the nurse handed me the milkshake. I slurped it right down. I couldn't understand why there was a sheriff standing at the door the whole time. I wasn't a criminal. Then they put ointment on my raw knuckles and wrapped gauze around them.

The doctor took me to another room and the sheriff followed us. On the way I saw all the news people with cameras and microphones jostling at the end of the corridor. What's the big deal? I told myself. I just couldn't admit what had really happened. It would crush me and I could never let anything ever crush me. Those news people were forcing me to acknowledge the whole ordeal, so I turned away.

The doctor X-rayed my right hand and the nurse stayed with me when he left to check the results.

You have a broken hand, he said when he got back.

I looked at my hand. The top bulged into a red mound. Trying to flex it was impossible and the pain immobilized my whole arm. I heard the sheriff's radio chirp—something about the rescue team needing ropes to get up the mountain. I thought of the chute—so steep it nearly pitched me backward as I hugged the ice. It seemed impossible to make it down that mountain with my hand like this. The doctor bent his ear toward the sheriff's radio while stealing a glance at my broken hand. Ever so slightly he recoiled and he looked spooked for a second. Then he smiled.

Time to put a cast on that hand, Norman, he said.

After the cast was on the nurse re-dressed my seared fingers with ointment and gauze, then wrapped an Ace bandage around the cast—it looked like a fatheaded club.

I was lost in thought—Sandra's wide-open eyes staring up at me, tiny chunks of sapphire, not brown like they were supposed to be. No matter how hard I pressed the blue out and pushed the brown in, the iris remained sapphire. A voice was directing somebody into my room. I slid off the bed. The door opened and my mom rushed up to me and her purse banged the linoleum floor as she kneeled and hugged me, her tears dripping onto my cheek. Her voice sputtered. They told me the search had been called off, she said.

My mom raked her fingers through my hair. Her eyes searched as if to make sure I was really there.

Then an hour later they called again and said, *A boy alleging to be from a plane crash showed up in Baldy Village.*

My mom clenched me tighter.

Nick came forward. He patted my back and told me he thanked God I was alive. I remembered the deal I had made—that if I made it down I'd believe in God—but it didn't seem like God had anything to do with my making it down. Instead I thanked my dad.

Did they get Dad yet? I said.

Nick glanced at my mom.

No, honey, she said. They found Sandra though.

Is she dead?

Yes.

I thought so, I said.

They said you covered her with twigs, said Nick.

Yeah. To keep her warm.

If you thought she was dead why did you cover her up? said Nick.

I furrowed my brow. Does he think I'm lying again?

What if she wasn't dead, I said.

Nick blinked as if having been slapped across the cheek. Uh-huh, he said.

There was a window in the room and I noticed it was dark. That was the last time I asked about my dad. No tears. I felt buffered, having replaced my eleven-year-old-boy skin with something thicker.

CHAPTER 39

THE NEXT MORNING Nick's face was swollen and his eyes were bloodshot, the way he looked after a big night of drinking. I was wheeled into a large room filled with reporters and cameras. My mom and I answered their questions. I told them that my dad taught me *never give up*. It was something Nick had said the night before and it sounded right so I said it.

After the interview we drove back to the Palisades, to the house my dad had bought on the edge of a canyon above the ocean. My hands were useless with the gauze and cast and my feet were still numb on the tips so I didn't get to go outside and play.

Eleanor came over that night. She rested in bed with me. My mom and Nick were very quiet upstairs. My legs were cramping and the pain made me squirm around. I couldn't sleep. I turned on the radio, which was tuned to a news channel. They were talking about the airplane crash. Two people were speculating about whether or not the plane could have been sabotaged by

an incensed element within the FBI. They talked about J. Edgar
Hoover's vindictiveness and how he had a lot of loyal lieutenants still high up in the FBI.

Hogwash, said Eleanor, turning the dial to a different station. They're always looking for conspiracies. People love bad
pretends.

My legs were knotting up, so she rubbed them out for me.
She had to massage my legs the entire night, talking me through
the pain, reading to me, making me feel safe. I knew my mom was
busy with Nick, discussing things, important things, I guessed.
As long as I had Eleanor, my other mother, I had what I needed.

I slept most of the following day. My mom made me whatever
kind of food I wanted and right after wolfing it down I'd fall
back to sleep.

On my second night home I woke up around 9:00 p.m. I lay
in bed for a while before I smelled the scent of weed coming
from upstairs. I heard my mom and Nick laughing. It was loud.
I called Eleanor from the phone beside my bed.

Please come over, I said.

When she showed up at the door my mom asked her what
she was doing. Eleanor told her that I had called.

Eleanor. I can handle it, said my mom.

I came upstairs and insisted that Eleanor stay. Nick and my
mom appeared paralyzed by my demand. I'm sure my bruised
sutured face, broken hand and gauze-covered fingers had dis-
armed them.

A few days later Grandma and Grandpa Ollestad arrived from
Puerto Vallarta. Grandma talked continually, as if deafening

herself against something wailing inside her. Grandpa was stoic as usual and his eyes were soft and stirring. They shone with tears that never dripped down his cheeks.

Aunts, uncles, and cousins gathered at my dad's cabin-house in Topanga Canyon. We all sat in the living room and they told stories about Dad. I went to my room and cried without all those sympathetic faces watching me.

Alone in my old room, I felt my chest begin to burn. The armor around me, the animal skin, was melting from the heat in my body. My tears seemed to come out of the hot space in my chest. The faster they spilled, the more out of control I felt.

You could easily turn into a weirdo. Watch out, I told myself. Don't fall apart.

Allowing my body to unclamp was too dangerous. The skin knitted me together. Kept me whole.

One more bad thing happens and you might lose it, I thought.

Timothy, the kid on my block who always stared at his feet, haunted me. I thought about him dragging around like a beaten dog, hiding behind his comic books, tripping over his feet as he scuttled away from the neighborhood boys throwing balls at him.

I stood up from my old bed and sucked up my pain. I wiped my cheeks and walked back into the living room with a smile, just like my dad would have.

Hundreds of people showed up to my dad's funeral at the Little Church of the Flowers. Many stood in the aisles and the crowd seeped out the doorways because the church only accommodated 250 people and there were no seats left. I cried every time somebody went to the podium and when Eleanor spoke she seemed far off in the distance. I kept blinking and the people around me appeared very close, then far away. I mentally shucked off these splintered images, reeling myself back to the steady world that I knew was right there.

They had to stop letting people talk because two hours had gone by and the church officials wanted to wind it down.

Uncle Joe, my dad's half brother, whose hotel we stayed at in Lake Tahoe, threw a party after the funeral. All my relatives danced to a live Dixieland band and they all said they thought it was what my dad would have wanted. He always hooted in powder—good or bad—and fought through storms and riptides, I thought, and played guitar even when the *vaqueros* despised him, transforming that hostile night into something beautiful.

I danced at the party too and it seemed like I was on an escalator moving on a different plane at a different pace, like there was no gravity holding me. Cousins, aunts and uncles moved with their feet on the ground—they had gravity. I seemed separated from everyone by thick glass and it made all sounds a din of noise and I told myself not to get creepy like that Timothy kid.

I stopped playing hockey, stopped surfing, and mostly just hung out with the neighborhood kids and hoped I wouldn't turn sullen and awkward. Instead I came down with a lot of sore throats and had to stay inside and alone several days a week. My body was not used to all that *hanging around* and my grief stayed crammed up inside me, with no outlet—except the sore throats.

That spring I got strep throat and a high fever, and it was Nick who nursed me back to health. He put his lips to my forehead to measure my temperature, and tenderly administered his Irish remedies, coming to my bed with a spoonful of warm water, plopping an aspirin in the water, and telling me how to drink it down while we watched it dissolve. As Nick prescribed, I let the aspirin bits catch in my throat. Amazingly it took most of the pain away. That evening he made a hot toddy—hot tea with shots of brandy, some lemon and honey. My mom saw him concocting the hot toddy in the kitchen and she deemed him Nurse Nick. When it was ready he brought a mug of it to my bedside. Then he rolled me up inside two comforters with only my head poking free like a sausage rolled up in a pancake. He carefully poured the hot toddy into my mouth and it burned my throat and stomach.

Nick told me that his mom used to nurse him and his brother and sisters back to health with hot toddies. She hated having to take care of us when we were sick, said Nick.

You mean she didn't want to? I strained to say.

God no, he said. She'd scowl at us if we seemed like we were coming down with something.

The hot toddy made me sweat before I even finished it. Nick tucked me in, making a big show of it—tucking the comforter under my ribs and thighs and feet. I fell right to sleep. When I woke up the next morning the comforters were soaked, my temperature was gone and my throat was just a little scratchy.

Thanks Nurse Nick, I said to him.

It was a relief to feel closer to him, but it seemed dangerous too.

At the end of June, I graduated from grammar school and Grandma Ollestad had pneumonia so I couldn't go to Mexico until later that summer. Nick said I had to get a job. Grandpa was in L.A., perhaps picking up special medicine for Grandma, and he informed me of a new diner across from Topanga Beach that he had stopped at while taking a cruise down the Coast Highway. So he drove me down there and I got a job as a food prepper, server and busboy. Grandpa left a few days later.

On a whim one day after work I crossed the Pacific Coast Highway and stood on the bluff above the converted lifeguard station. All the surf legends were hanging out on the sand in front of the station, and different-colored surfboards leaned against the bottom half of it, which was open on all four sides. The waves were small and I recognized Chris Rohloff, my old buddy who had surprised me in Mexico last summer. He was riding a sparkling green peeler, his front arm cocked at the elbow like a scarecrow. He was goofy-footed like me and I found myself going through the motions, pumping up and down to make the section. He rode the wave to the inside. In one motion he hopped off his board, snatched it up under his arm and danced from one slippery rock to the next all the way to the beach. Man he's gotten good, I thought.

I skidded down the dirt path winding around the succulents where I used to play hide-and-seek and onto the access road. I crossed a slab of concrete where the lifeguards parked their trucks and I realized it was our old garage, roofless and adrift in the sand.

I stepped off this relic and approached the lifeguard station. To the south the beach curved toward Santa Monica, where tall buildings stood behind the salty haze. My eyes lowered, settling on Bob Barrow's brick stairs climbing off the beach, the porch gone but the porch footings stabbing out of the sand, and up the dirt embankment to the access road. The stairs looked like a spine without a body. All along the beach columns of stairways lay like skeletons from another era against the ripped-apart embankment.

I thought of the ghost towns my dad and I had passed through and it hurt to imagine what this one used to be like.

I came to a standstill. The old days long gone percolated in dew across my eyes and it all dappled together like a pond reflection until Rohloff called my name.

Norm, he said.

I turned and blinked and the mist congealed into a clear picture.

Hey man. Where've you been? he said.

The bodies in the sand twisted around and a chorus greeted me. The ghost town came alive.

I don't know. Working, I said.

I stepped forward and slapped fives and brandished a hang-loose sign to each legend while the various girls and guys augmenting the scene looked on.

Shane told me I looked like I healed up pretty good, and I touched the indented scar on my chin. Trafton asked me if I was ready to surf again. I wondered how he knew I hadn't surfed in months. I nodded yes out of reflex. When Rohloff offered his board for a *go out* I used the excuse of not having trunks.

It seemed strange that I would come to the beach without trunks or a surfboard, so I explained that I worked across the street at the diner. Rohloff said it was good for lunch but everybody else said they liked George's Market better.

I took off my shoes, plopped on the sand and dug my toes in, listening to everybody talk surf. A swell was due in a couple days from south of Tahiti. Shane thought Catalina Island might block the waves, and I glanced southward as if assessing how the swells would hit Catalina, a smudge on the horizon. Within five minutes I was on the inside of the circle, chiming in at will, and I took off my shirt and felt the sting of the sun on my skin. An hour later I was running up the access road past Barrow's dilapidated landing and I was excited about tomorrow for the first time in months.

Our garage was at street level. I ran right up to the door, unlocked it and searched for my yellow-railed seven-foot-two surfboard that Dad had given me on my tenth birthday. I couldn't find it. So I walked down the stairs toward the house, which rested on the hillside below the garage. I looked in the storage space under the garage. It wasn't there. Sunny followed me around and whimpered and I knew she wanted to play so I took her into the canyon and threw the stick until she was panting hard.

I was consumed by the notion of surfing again. I worried about whether I would still be able to hop right up and make the drop and generate speed down the line.

When my mom returned from teaching summer school I skipped the hellos and asked where my board was.

Gosh I think it's in the garage somewhere, she said.

I looked in there, I said.

What about above. In the rafters?

Oh yeah.

I used the hood of my mom's VW to ladder myself to a rafter beam. I pulled myself up and crawled around in the dust and heat that had accumulated in the attic. In the back on top of boxes I found my board.

I hosed it off on the grass outside the front door and my mom asked me how it felt to see Topanga again.

Weird, I said.

She waited for me to say more and followed me to the kitchen. I grabbed a spatula to clean off the dirt-encrusted wax.

She followed me back outside.

Were all the guys there? she said.

Yeah.

Was it good to see them?

Yeah, I said.

I looked at her and her entire face opened up like she was feeling something pleasant touching her skin.

I hope I can still surf, I said.

It's like riding a bike, she said.

You used to surf, right?

Oh yeah, she said. Your dad got me out there almost every day one summer.

What happened? I said.

She stuttered.

Oh. You know. Winter came. It got cold. And the next summer you were born.

But didn't you want to keep surfing?

To tell you the truth, not really. I did it for your dad. Once we divorced I lost interest. She flipped her hair back and looked out at the ocean. He gave me lots of attention when we were surfing, she said.

Her longing for other forms of attention from my dad did not register. Instead the notion that Nick didn't surf either and that my mom had abandoned surfing, maybe even because Nick didn't do it, suddenly made surfing my one and only desire. It took me by the throat. Surfing would cut me free.

After work I walked out along the dirt knoll and came around the top of the point. I crossed the mouth of the creek, shored up now for lack of rain, and it was spawning green moss. Then the crew saw me and somebody whistled. It made me smile and my cheeks crinkled, sensitive from yesterday's sunburn.

I asked for a bar of wax and Shane himself rose and climbed

under the station and reached into the crossbeams under the top story and handed me a bar.

My secret stash, he said.

I waxed up my board and Shane said he remembered when my old man had bought the board for me.

It's a clean shape. Fast down the line, he said.

I nodded. For Shane to give me some of *his* wax and then compliment *my* board was a kind of achievement and I noticed some of the crew watching and I was as sure as ever that it was a big deal.

All the ceremonies were played out and there was no way to delay the inevitable anymore. Time to paddle. Rohloff picked up his board and said he'd come along.

We hoisted our boards and walked to the point. The tide was high and the waves gathered against the rock shelf and finally broke in a bundle of energy, unreeling like a beam of light running down the line.

It's only waist-high, I told myself.

Where's the take-off spot? I said.

He looked at me suspiciously. Right off the creek, he said.

A moment later Rohloff wasn't next to me anymore. He was leaning on his board stepping through the shallows.

There's a little channel through here, Norm.

I trotted back and hustled to get right in his trail. The channel was mostly sand with an occasional rock. My fin hit a rock and Rohloff told me to flip my board over. When the water came over our knees he righted his board and jumped on and paddled. I did the same. My shoulders cracked as if breaking through a dry husk and I labored to propel myself forward. By the time I made it to the take-off zone I was beat.

There was a lot of seaweed to wade through and I knew that would make it doubly hard to catch the waves. I sat up and looked toward the beach. The yellow submarine house used to be right there, I figured, eyeing the plot of dirty sand. I had watched the party from out here, over the backs of the swells. Dad had told me that one day I'd realize how great it was, how lucky I was, and be glad he made me learn to surf.

A set, Norm, said Rohloff.

I swung my board around, nearly tipping over, and followed Rohloff, hoping he'd steer me into the right spot for take-off. He spun his board like a turret and dropped forward and his arms stroked around twice, rising gracefully out of the water. An instant later he popped to his feet and glided below the wave, then his scarecrow arm posted above the lip.

Just in time I became aware of the next wave and cranked my nose into the pitching face and sliced through. The cold water snapped my senses to the fore and I tingled. The air was crisp and my ears gurgled with saltwater. The seaweed stench seemed to drive me toward the next swell even though my shoulder muscles threatened to rip from the bone. I coughed and grunted and tore against the water, driven by those familiar sensations.

There was a lot of wasted energy, lurching and jerking, before I somehow scratched into the wave. When I stood up my legs quivered and I had to steady my labored breathing. I used my entire weight to lean back and scoop the nose of the board out of the trough at the bottom. Then I tottered to one side just enough to steer the board off the bottom and down the line. I leveled into the face and the lip was curling in front of me. I gyrated, rocking from rail to rail, pumping my knees. I just started doing it. With each pump the board jetted. Suddenly I was screaming like a bottle rocket, hooked into some invisible flow. And like that, in the blink of an eye, I was dancing again above the earth in that old magnificent world.

The wave closed out in front of the station and I kicked over the back. They all hooted from the beach. An older guy with a mustache and curly hair made me look twice. The second time I felt my eyes sting and my face seemed to crumble. Dropping my head, I shuffled my board around and paddled toward the point, coughing and gagging on the tears and mucus.

I paused and drifted shy of the point. Rohloff kept glancing at me. I angled away from him.

You okay, Norm? he called out.

I raised my arm. This rocked me to the opposite side and I searched beneath the surface. The sparkling sediments rained down past the tiny bubbles leaking from the rocks below. The perfume in my nose and the gurgling in my ears. Home.

If it wasn't for your dad I might not be surfing right now, said Rohloff when I paddled back to the point. I for sure wouldn't be as good.

Good thing, huh? I said.

He tipped his head up and down. Lovin' it, he said.

By summer's end I had my own money and my own set of friends and was so out of the loop with my mom and Nick that I hadn't realized Nick had moved out. Even though I stayed at Eleanor's some nights, she never mentioned it. It wasn't until my first day of junior high that I asked my mom where Nick was.

He moved to the beach, she said.

Good, I said.

I told him he can come back when he stops drinking, she said.

That'll never happen, I thought, and I nodded.

She tried to look strong. But I thought she would let him come back, after some excuse, and I refused to stand there and pretend otherwise, so I bolted.

. . .

On my first day at Paul Revere Junior High one of the eighth-grade boys, a surfer named Rich, recognized me from Topanga Beach. Apparently he was out surfing one day that summer and had seen how all the legends watched out for me and how every once in a while they let me take a set wave. Rich befriended me because I was anointed in a club that I suddenly realized was spectacularly cool even beyond the oasis of Topanga Beach. By day two I was hanging with Rich and the popular crew. They had long hair and burned skin and always wore shorts and ragged shirts. I fit right in like a jigsaw piece, folding me back into the regular world again. You were right Dad, thanks for making me surf.

A week later, I woke in the night and there was a strange glow out my bedroom window. I went upstairs and into my mom's room and outside her glass door I saw tongues of fire.

Wake up! I yelled.

I was naked and when her eyes opened I turned away before she saw the three pubic hairs sprouting out. I ran downstairs and put on some boxers. My mom waited, urging me to forget about the boxers, she had a towel for me. Then we ran out of the house together. I reached into the storage area under the garage to retrieve my surfboard. She yelled at me from the stairs, but I wasn't going to let it burn. Feeling the heat of the fire on my back, I hauled my board up the stairs, past the garage and onto the street. Mom knocked on a neighbor's door and they called the fire department.

Nick showed up a half hour later. The whole roof was burned and the drywall on the top floor was charred from the heat. The fire chief said that embers from a fire earlier that night about a mile north, carried by the Santa Ana winds, had probably landed on our roof. Because our roof was made of old shingles, he said, it caught fire easily.

We had to move into a house about two miles away, across Sunset Boulevard, for six months. The first night there my mom mentioned *puberty*, and I realized she had seen me naked the night of the fire and I was embarrassed. Then she asked me if I felt different.

No, I said, unwilling to admit that over the last few months I had often been surprised by jolts of aggression. Outbursts of anger that never quite made it out of my body. I'm going to bed, I said.

During our first week at the new house Nick came around. It wasn't clear whether or not he had quit drinking and I didn't ask my mom. I steered clear of him and he steered clear of me.

Around this time one of the girls from seventh grade invited the surfer crew to a party on a Saturday night. My weekend curfew was 10:00. I came home at 10:30 and my mom was upset, worried. She threatened to ground me. I shut my bedroom door on her and opened *Surfer Magazine* and thought about surfing and one of the girls from the party named Sharon who kept talking to me. My phone rang and I picked it up and it was Sharon. She asked me if I had fun at the party. It was great, was all I could come up with. Then she asked me if I was going to masturbate. I didn't know what to say. I told her I had never done it. She scoffed and said I was lying. I swore to her that I never had. She sounded excited and invited me over on Sunday.

Cool, I said.

She told me her address and I found a pen and wrote it on my hand.

Good night, she said in a sultry voice.

I couldn't sleep. Even though I knew about sex, had seen it all around me on Topanga Beach, I wasn't sure if I should be masturbating or not, or really how to do it. How could I be so out of it?

My date commenced with Sharon stealing her parents' Mercedes and driving us to Westwood. She was only thirteen, so driving a Mercedes along Sunset Boulevard with the windows down and Blondie blaring made her the coolest chick in the world. Sharon gave me my first ever handjob on Makeout Mountain, providing a helpful model for how to masturbate in the future. By the time she parked in front of my house, scraping the hubcap against the sidewalk, it was forty minutes past my curfew.

I ran up the brick stairs of our temporary house, a single-story stucco with plastic awnings. I tried to open my bedroom window but it was locked. I circled to the side of the house and climbed onto the back porch. The sliding-glass door to the porch was cracked. I slipped inside.

I tiptoed to my bedroom door and was not halfway there when my mom opened her bedroom door.

You're busted, Norman.

I'm getting some milk, I said.

I don't think so. Go to bed and we'll deal with it in the morning.

Over breakfast my mom informed me that I was grounded the following weekend.

That's bullshit, I said.

Another word and it's two weekends.

We'll see, I said.

She glared at me and I scoffed and chomped on my cereal. I slurped it down in one gulp, dropped the bowl in the sink, grabbed my skateboard and left.

Do you have your lunch? called my mom.

I ignored her and skateboarded as fast as I could to catch the bus to Paul Revere Junior High.

Nick was in the kitchen with my mom when I got home from school. He eyed me with a puckered face. I aimed for my room.

Norman, said my mom.

I stopped. What?

You were forty-five minutes late last night, said Nick.

The bus was late, I said.

You lie without hesitation, said Nick. It's become second nature, Jan.

Mellow out, I said to him.

He shook his head.

You're goin' down a bad road, Norman, he said.

Whatever, I said.

Sharon's mother called me today, said my mom.

My insides dropped and went fluttering down my legs and I was hollow.

I shot her a *so-what* face.

Did you or did you not take Sharon's mother's car? said Nick.

I wasn't driving, I said.

She's thirteen years old, said my mom.

I told her not to do it.

But you got in the car, said Nick.

She was leavin' no matter what.

You'd jump off a bridge if she told you to? said Nick.

I missed the bus. I was late.

They noticed the car was gone at 7:30, said Nick. You got home at 10:45.

I didn't do anything. I just got a ride, I said. She was going anyways.

The fucking denial, the lack of any shred of compunction, is really fucking sickening, said Nick.

I shrugged. Whatever.

His hand was around my neck in a flash and I was tripping backward. I grabbed his forearm and he lifted me off the ground and slammed me against the refrigerator. I slid to the ground and the floor knocked the wind out of me. His eyes were red with throbbing vessels and his face was purple and his fingernails dug into my neck. I had a clear shot at him—my arms free at my sides, his face unguarded. But my biceps turned to weeds. I was afraid to fight back.

Let go. I'm choking, I said.

Let go of him, Nick!

You give me a go-fuck-yourself look again and I'm going to wipe it right off your face.

Okay, I sputtered and nodded.

He unclenched his fingers. I breathed again.

He stood.

A nice little family discussion, he said sarcastically, and he and my mom both laughed. It was clear that she had aligned herself with him again.

Are you okay? said my mom.

I ignored her and stood up and stared out the window.

Your mother asked you a question, Norman, said Nick.

Yeah I'm great, I said staring out the window.

Okay. Well. You're grounded for two weeks, said my mom. No going out. You have to come home right after school. Got it?

What about surfing? I said.

No surfing either.

I turned and glared at my mom.

Why would you think it would be okay to go *surfing* if you're *grounded*? said Nick.

I wanted to tell him to go fuck himself. However, he was correct—if you're grounded it doesn't make sense to be able to go surfing.

This will help you finally learn about consequences, he said. That your actions have consequences. Welcome to the NFL.

It was a peculiar thing to say but I fully understood it. I even smirked.

I served out my sentence for tardiness and lying and the winter turned to spring and we moved back to the house on the edge of the canyon and it seemed like all I thought about was surfing and sex—though I was still a virgin. Then right before spring break Sharon left me for an eighth-grader. She called me aside one day, explaining that he was really just more her type. I walked away weak-legged and I thought I might cry as I stole into the bathroom. I did not love her and I couldn't understand why it hurt so much. I locked myself in a stall so that nobody would see me like this.

I was kissing Sharon yesterday and today she's gone. I wanted to touch her again, lose myself against her body. Our make-out sessions were suddenly blissful moments that I longed for. I had told her things that only Eleanor knew. My mind raced, searching for somebody to fill in for Sharon—Sharon under my body, breathing into my ear while I kissed her neck. Then she vanished, abandoned me, and I was free falling. My knees hit the bathroom floor and I spit into the toilet on the verge of vomiting.

I wiped my mouth. All the aggression that had been mounting over the previous couple months erupted. I turned and side-kicked the stall door. I kicked it and kicked it until the lock busted and dangled from the door. Moving to the sink, I felt looser. Not so jammed up anymore. I splashed water on my face and cooled down. As I made my way back to the hangout spot by the cafeteria I thought about beating up Nick.

On Friday night I skateboarded to a party with the surfer crew and they got into a fight with some jocks, reminding me that I used to be a jock. I wanted to hit somebody—it would feel good, doling out a little punishment and not just taking it all the time. Instead I watched from the sidelines.

It was a weekend and I had just come back from the beach when my mom told me that Grandma Ollestad had lung cancer. I touched my neck remembering my sore throats and I thought that maybe I could get throat cancer.

She didn't smoke, did she? I said.

Never. That's what's so strange about it, she said. She's going to Tijuana for a special treatment they don't offer in the States. I thought we'd drive down and visit her next weekend.

Okay, I said.

I sat down on the couch and stared out the window. Grandma's black lungs crawled with cancer-worms and I zoomed toward the ocean below as if tumbling down the hillside. When I looked at my mom again she appeared to be scattered around the living room as if I were in a house of mirrors. I closed my eyes and wondered what the hell was wrong with me.

The following Saturday we loaded Nick's station wagon and I put my surfboard in last so it would not get dinged by the suitcases.

You're not bringing your fucking surfboard, said Nick.

Why not? I said.

We're going down there to spend time with your grandmother, not to surf. Take it out.

I'm not going to surf the whole time. Just after we've been there all day. Just in case it's good.

No. Absolutely not.

Nick, said my mom. Let him bring the board. We're not going to be in the hospital all day every day.

His grandmother is dying, Jan. This might be the last time he sees her. He can manage not to surf for two days.

He turned to me.

This is not about you, Norman. It's about your grandmother. I know that's hard for you to comprehend.

I get it, I said. I just want to have the board in case there's some extra time. What's wrong with that?

Because it's not about that. You have to learn to think of other people sometimes without putting your selfish needs into the equation.

He grabbed the board and walked it to the side door of the garage, unlocked the door and went inside with it.

What an asshole, I said to my mom.

Just let it go, Norman, she said.

This will be good for you, Norman, Nick said with a grin as we drove away.

I wanted to slug him. It brought me back to those days on Topanga Beach when I wished I were bigger and stronger. I had always believed that I'd be able to whip him by the time I turned thirteen and now my thirteenth birthday was a month away and I wasn't close.

· · ·

Grandma's silver curls were flat on one side and she had tubes in her arms and her eyes were sunken back in their sockets and colorless behind a glassy film. Eleanor was there with Lee and she cried when she saw me. An aunt or uncle offered me a seat and I collapsed into it. Grandpa sat on a rickety chair beside the hospital bed and watched Grandma. He was slouched and his face was haggard.

Somebody said, Little Norman's here, and Grandma sat up. She found me and her eyebrows perked. Her pupils were so dilated that she looked blind. The rest of her face, apart from the eyebrows, was limp and expressionless. Then she shifted her attention across the room and spoke toward the empty corner. It was pure babble. Her arms rose and she gestured and babbled.

The morphine makes her hallucinate, explained Eleanor.

I watched her moan and talk to different imaginary things. Then she fell back on the pillow and stared at the ceiling, motionless. Grandpa put his hand on her arm and she stared at the ceiling with a clinched mouth and nobody spoke.

She's kinda like Sandra was, I thought. Her body is there but her mind is gone.

When we left for the night I kissed and hugged Grandpa and he was all skin and bones. I waited with Eleanor outside the room while my mom and Nick said their good-byes. I asked her how Grandma could get lung cancer if she never smoked and was so healthy.

Grief, said Eleanor. If you push it down it can grow into something toxic like cancer. Your father was her masterpiece.

In our hotel room I thought about how it would have killed my dad if I had died and he had survived, just like it was killing Grandma. We were staying out by Rosarita Beach and I heard waves crashing in the distance and I wished I could escape out into them.

After a second day at the hospital it was time to say good-bye to Grandma. She had been lucid all morning and when I hugged her I felt her muscles and bones vised together and I knew she was in excruciating pain and that the moment I left they would shoot her up with morphine and she'd relax and hallucinate again. That was the last time I ever saw her.

On the drive home I decided there was no God and that we were all on our own here.

The following weekend I went to a party at a house in Brentwood with a big pool and a tennis court and its own movie theater. I kicked my skateboard onto the brick flower planter in the driveway and grinded my trucks along the edge, chipping off slivers of brick.

You totally thrashed their wall, said one of the guys I was rolling with.

I glanced back at the slivers on the ground.

Yep, I said, feeling that same sense of relief as when I broke the stall door.

The gang let out a nervous laugh. I led them around the back, through a gate and onto a lush green lawn with rolling mounds and flowers and roses along the edges. We marched around the corner and the entire party—maybe twenty-five kids—turned around to see us. Missy the hostess was lounging poolside with her set of rich girls on gigantic pink towels. She lifted her Ray-Bans and waved only her fingers, ambivalent about our presence.

Immediately I met each and every pair of male eyes staring at us. I wanted to punch someone again. Feel myself unload. It seduced me. I scowled at the boys, hoping for a scowl back. There were no takers and I strutted to the cooler and got a beer.

We sat on our skateboards, kicking aside the chairs and benches—a rebuke of civilization—and sipped our beers, commenting on the digs. Where a half-pipe skateboard ramp would go, or if we should drain the pool and skate it.

Missy stood up and straightened her bikini and waddled over.

You guys need to promise to be mellow, okay? said Missy.

Can we drain your pool? I said.

Norman. No way. I'll call the rent-a-cops if you mess with the pool. I'm not kidding.

Where're your parents? I said.

They're out of town, but the housekeeper's here, so . . .

So we can totally rage, I said.

That got a big laugh and some howls of enthusiasm.

One of the rich girls whom I had never seen before made a comment. I whipped around and confronted her.

What'd you say?

The girl was pretty. Hair perfect. Skin even and supple. She wore a ridiculous gold dress and swanky gold sandals and clutched a frilly handbag to her bosom. She spoke with an accent—English maybe—and tightened her mouth into a sphincter when I addressed her.

You're rude and immature, she said with her nose literally in the air.

Fuck being mature, I said. That's boring.

What's wrong with you? she said.

I opened my mouth to respond and I saw all those kids staring at me. I stumbled on my words and it seemed like everyone could see how weird and sad I really was and it scared me.

I grabbed her arm, tugged her off the lounge chair and flung her into the pool.

She came up with her hair in her face and her dress billowed across the surface and her arms got caught in it and I thought I'd have to dive in and save her. Half the party was laughing.

Several girls and a boy went to her rescue and helped her out of the pool. Her eyes and nose were covered by wet limp hair and her mouth trembled. Her nipples were exposed through the wet gold material.

Missy and company took the girl inside and the party died. I was afraid to make eye contact with anyone so I opened another beer and skated onto the tennis court and did layback tail-slides on the smooth concrete. Thinking of that girl sobbing, her limp dress clinging to her like cellophane, triggered a strange empty-ing sensation in my face—it was eroding into a skull. My skin seemed to crawl off me, leaving the sinewy muscles and tendons of my entire body fully exposed. A grotesque, mutilated boy. I wondered what my dad would think of me now.

Missy appeared, trailing two rent-a-cops. It was time to leave. We gathered our boards and I flipped the cops off and we ran out the gate.

We rode the bus to Westwood and picked a fight with some Emerson Junior High kids. One of our crew got pinned in a tele-phone booth by three big Emerson guys. The rest of my crew was busy with their own battles. Again I found myself on the sidelines and I remembered a man at my dad's funeral describ-ing how a mob of Stanford football fans had jumped him at a game, and how my dad was the only guy that charged in there to help him. I charged headlong into the phone booth, ramming two big guys in the back with my skateboard. It broke them apart and somehow we scrambled away just as cop sirens were approaching.

The crew split up and I hid atop Makeout Mountain, then

took the back streets to Sunset Boulevard and rode the bus home. I made it just before my curfew. Nick was up watching TV and asked me how I got the cut on my nose.

Fell skating, man, I said.

I went downstairs and looked in the mirror. I couldn't remember getting hit in the nose. My eyes looked tired and the dark circles were like a sick boy's and my body vibrated and I told myself that rich chick got what she deserved. Still, her quivering mouth and the way she stumbled toward the house in her wilted dress bothered me and I turned away from my reflection in the mirror.

When I awoke the next morning I was still on edge. I went to Topanga and paddled out, not saying hello to anyone. I dropped in on every surfer except the legends and Rohloff. I slugged a big kid named Benji in the face when he splashed water in my eyes after I snaked his wave. He grabbed my hair and dunked me under. Shane called the kid off. Benji let me up and I told him to go fuck himself and paddled to the point.

We got your back, Norman, said Shane. But you might want to tone it down, you know.

I nodded.

The aggression and anger seemed to enfold and redouble inside me and it made me jittery and I kept blowing the waves, digging a rail or overextending my turns. Benji made a point to laugh loudly each time. I reminded myself that he could not punch me even though I deserved it and I relished that injustice.

I turned thirteen and that summer I spent half my time in fist-fights. I got my ass kicked fairly often, and the blows to my nose or jaw or ribs were strangely gratifying. Even in defeat I always made sure I got a couple licks in that the other guy wouldn't soon forget. Sometimes getting whupped made me feel tougher than doing the whupping. I knew I could take anything and that made me feel like the winner in spite of my blackened eye or bloodied nose.

That fall I did poorly in school and Nick grounded me for a month.

One afternoon while I read surf magazines in my prison cell Nick came home early from work. I heard him banging around in the living room and then he called out my name. The blinds were drawn and there was a projector set up on the coffee table. Nick told me to sit down on the couch and watch the screen in front of the TV. He flipped a switch and the projector chugged and spit out a beam of light. On the screen appeared a Pop Warner football game. Nick had hired an editor to assemble a highlight reel of all my best plays—tackling big fullbacks that had darted through the defensive line into the backfield. Catching a pass over the middle as a monstrous linebacker engulfed me, the ball still in my arms when he pounded me into the grass. A quick shot of my dad eating peanuts in the stands with the sports section folded in a rectangle triggered a searing pain that burned a hole in my chest. I had to close my eyes until the ache went away.

When the reel tailed out Nick and I reminisced about me hiding fishing weights in my jockey cup during the weigh-in, about some of the dangerous neighborhoods that we played games in, and the various idiosyncrasies of the coaches and players.

You'll have this film to look back on forever, he said.

And I compared how I was then to how I felt now. I was callused and irritable these days, brooding. Who was that sweet-natured kid on the screen? What happened to him? Like most things that made me uncomfortable, though, I shrugged it off.

Rohloff called to give me surf reports and I read surf magazines to try to quench my hunger. After school I was pretty bored just loafing around the house, so I decided to fix the dings in my surfboard—at least I'd get to touch it. I fished out the can of resin and catalyst from the storage space under the garage and saw a cardboard box labeled Little Norman in the back corner.

I dragged it out and opened it up. I unearthed newspaper clippings, then yearbooks, then my Murcher Kurcher stories, and finally old photographs of me playing hockey, surfing Mexico, ski racing, me and Dad skiing St. Anton together, and me, as a baby, riding on my dad's back while he surfed. Mom told me she had come home from grocery shopping to discover me and Dad out in the surf. I went buzzeerk, she said. How could you be so careless with his little body? she screamed at my dad.

I dropped the photograph and tears pressed against the back of my eyes. I stooped and pushed the tears back. You're not some wimp that can't handle what happened, I told myself.

I called Sunny over and hugged her and rubbed her belly. She flopped onto her back and wiggled around in canine bliss.

I'm happy like you, I said.

Then I threw the stick as far as I could, and she went bounding down the canyon.

I put the photos back in the box, then the other stuff, and one of the newspaper clippings caught my eye: a *Los Angeles Times* black-and-white photograph of me sitting in a wheelchair with bandages all over my swollen face, a black eye and a bulkily wrapped right hand.

Already it seems like a dream, I thought. Like it happened to somebody else.

I sighed and something kicked up in my throat and scorched my rib cage and I had to sit down with my back against the house.

It's cool, I told myself. You're not messed up. You're okay.

I was supposed to be tough because I made it down that mountain. The dark feelings swirling and clawing inside me were something that I would just have to get over. Dad got over his hurt feelings. Shook them off. Moved on. Bad stuff just had to be reframed. I knew how to do that. And I read the article below the photo as if to prove how *okay* I was.

We decided we had to move or freeze to death. . . . My eyes stuttered on this sentence. I tried to push the onslaught of images aside, but I couldn't. I was back on the mountain, telling Sandra we had to go. She didn't want to go. But I made her go. Then she slipped and I reached out too far, miscalculated, and she disappeared into the mist.

My head and heart clenched, fending off spurts of pain. I rubbed my back against the house and it cut into my skin and I kept rubbing and had to force myself to stop. Settle down man.

My throat got thick so I drank water from the kitchen sink. It washed right through me and seemed to settle like everything else down in my feet. I splashed water on my face but I was still groggy. I hiked down the stairs and my thighs ached. I crawled into bed and fell asleep.

I woke up with a fever. Sandra might have lived if I let her stay under that wing.

I picked up an empty glass next to my bed and threw it at the wall. It shattered across my desk.

I stared at my knuckles, where the scar tissue was raised as if the skin had permanently blistered.

I twisted off the bed. Stop thinking about it.

I swept the glass slivers off the desk into the wastebin. Some spilled into a partially open drawer. I opened the drawer wide to get to the glass. Staring up at me was the plastic Indian that Dad had bought me in Taos.

I remembered that I used to look at it and think that if my dad ever dies then I want to die too.

He got killed taking me skiing, I said to the Indian.

I shut the drawer and went outside. I stuffed the newspaper clippings back into the box, closed the flaps and wedged it back into the corner under the garage. I had the flu for a week.

News of a big winter swell came via several phone calls from the school crew and Rohloff. I was finally over my fever and the descriptions of perfect peaks and juicy bowls and radical turns fueled my passion all week and by Thursday evening I was in a coiled frenzy.

My mom made honey-baked chicken, wild rice, and salad—her specialty—and I waited in my room until it was served, not wanting to have an outburst. After dinner I cleaned the dishes and then walked into the living room and addressed my mom and Nick, who were watching the news.

Look, I said. You have to understand.

I opened my hands as if holding a beach ball.

Man, I just need to surf, I said. It's like the thing that makes my heart pump, it's essential to what I am, and if I can't do it I can't function. I just feel dead inside and it's horrible.

Sunny was absorbing my every word and I pointed to her.

Imagine taking her stick away. No more retrieving. That would kill her. It's totally against her nature. Surfing is my retrieving. I don't need anything else. No friends or parties. I won't even hang out at the beach. I just need to be in that water, man, or I'm going to shrivel up.

Nick was leaning back on the couch and he was totally engrossed.

Please, Nick, I said.

Jesus Christ what a speech, said Nick, to my surprise. How can I say no? You know Norman if you put 10 percent of that kind of effort and passion into school, or anything, you could do great things. Really thrive.

Oh man. Thanks Nick, I said. Can you give me a ride in the morning before school? There's a pumping swell.

Well. I'm not working, he said. You know it's supposed to rain. Right?

I don't care, I said.

All right. I'll wake you up at 5:30.

Killer. Thanks.

I woke on my own at 5:15. The rain thumped out an incessant staccato on the plastic awning. Last night I had loaded my board and wetsuit into Nick's station wagon, so all I had left to do was throw down some cereal. Nick was making coffee in the kitchen.

You still want to go? he said.

Totally.

I was so excited that I couldn't eat more than one spoonful.

Nick put on a parka and a yellow rain slicker over it and a wool cap. I wore trunks and a sweatshirt and flip-flops.

You're going to get sick just wearing that, he said.

I'm going surfing anyway, I said.

He thought about it. You got a point, he said.

He blasted the station wagon's heater and I was sweating by the time we parked on the bluff overlooking Topanga Beach. The rain splattered the windshield and the trail to the beach was a mudslide. I studied the ocean. The wind and the swells and the globs of rain blurred together and out of nowhere white ribbons sprang from the blur and moved down the point.

Should we get the hell out of here? said Nick.

It's offshore, I said, watching the wind bend the fronds toward the ocean, which meant the wind was sweeping up the faces of the waves, smoothing them out.

I felt him looking at me. I glanced over. His face was buried in layers of wool and plastic, oval-framed like a nun in a frock. His stories of getting kicked out of several Catholic schools and getting punished by the nuns came to mind.

I reached back and brought my wetsuit into the front seat. I stripped down and tucked into the tight black rubber.

This seems like an awfully stupid idea, Norman, he said.

Why?

Why? It's raining like a frickin' hurricane and it's freezing. You can't see the waves. Plus there's probably a motherfucker of a rip current out there.

I looked out the window again. Diaphanous coils of white-wash moved behind the rain and I imagined the offshore winds feathering back the crest of a wave and felt the exhilaration of the ride.

Looks fantastic, I said.

He did a double take and we both knew that's exactly what my dad would have said. I realized then, like a shade zipping up on a giant window, that Nick respected my dad a lot, and that Nick probably wanted to be as good a dad as Big Norm. He seemed trapped in the car by the storm and for the first time in my entire life I felt sympathetic toward him.

I didn't want him to see this in my face, so I ducked down and put my booties on. When I sat up Nick was watching the ocean. His eyes roved the scene as if it were something awesome and too dangerous to mess with. I followed his gaze outside. Behind the thrashing rain, at the bottom of the mudslide, a few duck-dives away, was a paradise for those willing to fight through the storm.

I opened the door and the rain pelted me in the face, heavier than I expected. I took a hold of my old seven-foot-two, the yellow rails looked like dirty water in the pale light, and I shut the door with my foot. I crouched at the top of the path, then skimmed down on my booties and ass.

I ran up the point and saw Shane on a wave. It was over his head, big and gaping, and I was scared yet so desperate for a ride that I charged right in. The creek was running fast and it whisked me into the waves. I dove under the whitewash and paddled and negotiated the logs and tumbleweeds and garbage trapped in the break line between the creek current and the ocean current. It dragged me southward as if I were a twig and by the time I was outside the break I was halfway down the cove, past Barrow's brick stairs. They hung down the embankment, just a red smudge trail behind the streaks of rain.

I dug my arms deep into the water and my fingers were numb and wouldn't stay together, making them porous oars. I used everything I had just to get to the point.

Shane and Rohloff and one other guy I didn't know were out.

Hey, Little Norm, said Shane. The crew will be out soon, better get it now.

Totally, I panted.

It was hard to judge the surf because the offshore wind swirled the rain into patterns that looked like waves on the horizon. Rohloff stayed on his stomach, so I did too. We did not talk and just watched Shane. He paddled up the point against the current and we followed.

It caught us all by surprise and was eight feet tall. The wind held it up just in time for us to puncture the belly. The next wave was bigger and hidden by the first wave's blowback, coming out of the sky like a big-winged bird eclipsing the light and making it ten shades darker. The leading edge of the lip hit the middle of my back and bounced me off my board and the follow-through drilled me down into blackness. I rolled and told myself to rag-doll. I hoped I wouldn't hit a rock. When I came up my board was no longer on the end of my leash and I was in front of the lifeguard station, a hundred yards from the point.

I swam for the shore and the current dragged me south. The tide was high enough that I was able to flatten my body and ride a shore-pounder over the rocks.

I scanned the cove for my board. Then I saw Nick in his yellow rain slicker and umbrella up by the lifeguard station. My board was at his feet and he waved to me. I waved back.

I jogged into the wind and was panting by the time I reached him.

You had enough? he said.

My arms were noodles. My head was light and my dizziness made white gaps in his face. I shook my head and picked up my board. Without looking at him I jogged up the point. I tied what was left of my leash to the leash-plug and made three knots. I knew it would not hold if a big one hit me, so I would not be able to let go and dive deep because the leash would break and I'd have to swim in that current again, more tired than before.

I fought through the walls of whitewash and wished I had more food in my stomach. I ended up south of Barrow's again. I took ten strokes, rested, and took ten more. The current was setting me back five strokes per rest. I decided to go slower but not stop. Twenty minutes later I made it to the point. Shane and Trafton were the only guys out.

Where's Rohloff? I said.

Maybe that last set kinda worked him, said Shane.

I searched the inside and could not find him. All I saw was Nick's yellow figure on the sand. Thinking about him saying *You had enough?* made me determined to ride these big waves. Some-how if I didn't, Nick would be right about my character. I had given him this power and so I needed to reclaim it.

I paddled up the point, farther than Shane and Trafton. I knew they thought I was going too deep. I didn't look back and kept my eyes on the miasma of wind and water blurring the horizon.

It came and I paddled for it. Trafton and Shane yelped to rouse my courage. I got under the peak and turned, pointing the crown of my head into the offshore wind. I squinted to see through the sweeps of rain. The lip of the wave in front of me was sheared by the wind. I was choking on its blowback so I closed my mouth.

The tail of my board kicked up and I was going straight down and I jumped to my feet. The wind got under my board and I leaned on my front foot and broke the pocket, only to nose-dive. I stamped hard on the tail and yawed the nose loose. I was only halfway down the face and the wave was already leaning over me. The wind got under my board because it was skewed a bit and the offshore wind scraping up the face nearly blew me over the lip. Just in time I worked the rail down under the crest and suddenly airdropped onto the face again. This threw me back and the nose jerked up like a motorbike doing a wheelie, so I swung my arms around to keep from pitching off the tail. I had lost speed and the wave face heaved and expanded, about to swallow me. Frantically I gyrated and pumped, arms winging up and down. I ducked to avoid the falling lip just as the rails bit and my board responded. A few more pumps and the board began skipping across the surface, bouncing hard, and I bent my knees to absorb the turbulence and steadied her in the pocket.

I started working the board up and down despite the risk of getting too high up the face and getting pitched. That got me hauling ass, the offshore wind like a jet stream under my board. The section was relentless and the lip nearly decapitated me again, inciting a moment of doubt. I fought it off though by pumping even harder, and the propulsion was like a bobsled getting hurled through a concave track. I felt the wave's power root into me as if I grew out of the wave, and I locked into sync with her and suddenly she was easy to ride. Together we soared strong and free.

Rohloff was sitting on the sandbank and he ran down and slapped me five as I came ashore.

Insane ride, Norm, he said.

I hooted and he patted me on the back.

Come on. Let's get some more, I said.

He grabbed his board and we jogged up the beach.

See that one? I said when we passed Nick.

Nick nodded and I knew that I had done something he could never do, that he was too afraid to do. And I understood that riding waves made me feel things he could never feel. I paddled back out, strong and brave and a part of something that lifted me above all the shit.

My fingers were too numb to open the car door and Nick had to reach across the seat and open it from the inside. He had towels down over the vinyl and told me to get in. I put my hands against the blasting heaters and Nick put the car in reverse.

You got guts, kid, he said as he backed the car up.

Thanks for letting me go, I said.

It would be a lot easier if you didn't lie, Norman.

I know, I said. And it would be a lot easier if you didn't drink.

His eyes slanted hard and one side of his mouth curved.

What can I say, he said. You're right. When you're right you're right.

I watched the waves trail away from us below the highway.

Nick stopped drinking, going cold turkey, and soon afterward Grandma Ollestad died. Nick drove the three of us to her funeral. The service was in the same little church as my dad's funeral, about an hour away from the Palisades. Everyone spoke about how kind and giving and full of vitality Grandma had been and they mentioned my dad sometimes and I winced at the thought of him watching me these days, so spiteful and so blind to the beauty all around. As if he were hovering overhead, I told him that I was getting better. Did you see me surfing the other day?

On the way home from the funeral I kept thinking about Grandpa. He stood with a very straight back and when everybody gathered outside the church he listened carefully to each consoling relative. He only spoke a couple of times and his words were concise and poetic—like music or colors that send you upward. I thought about how his eyes were the same blue starbursts as my dad's and mine and I thought about how my dad would be very saddened by Grandma's death but not paralyzed by the grief, and I imagined him playing guitar for everyone outside the church.

We were driving down the freeway, Nick at the wheel, and I started to compare my dad's fluidity to Nick's jerky body language. Nick wrestled with each social interaction and at the funeral he sighed a lot and belted out hardened proclamations about death and life and so on. He grated against things, in a fever, compared to how I imagined my dad acting—an enchanter. Nick's pinched red face and Dad's wide smile juxtaposed in my mind.

As we came through the McClure tunnel onto the Coast Highway Nick spoke about being a good person, responsibility, hard work and honesty. He used words like *colossal* and *catastrophic* as if we were about to go off to war and this was our pep talk. Instead we arrived in the sleepy Palisades on a windless, cloudless Saturday afternoon.

I wandered down the stairs lost in my observations and comparisons and saw the ocean lined with swells stacked to the horizon. Grandpa, Eleanor and Lee were on their way over and I was afraid to ask if I could go surfing.

The next day I hung out with Grandpa over at Eleanor's house and nobody talked much.

Then in the afternoon Grandpa said, I have to fix the roof, and got in his car and drove back to Vallarta.

The following weekend I was doing my chores around the house and I noticed the waves picking up. I waited another hour to make sure the swells were not an anomaly. When they kept getting bigger and bigger I decided to take the 3:30 bus down to Topanga Beach. Nick and my mom had gone out to run errands and before they had left Nick reminded me that Sunny had been chasing coyotes into the canyon, which was a trap, and that our new policy was to put her inside or on the upstairs porch in the afternoon before it got dark so she wouldn't get lured into the coyotes' ambush.

No problem, I had said.

I reminded myself to put her inside while I made a melted cheese sandwich and Rohloff called from the phone booth at Topanga and said, It's goin' off the Richter. I got so excited that I just grabbed my gear and ran to the bus stop, inundated with visions of my board stabbing the lip and cutbacks and me riding inside a tube.

When I stepped off the bus a four-wave set was reeling in. The legends were in the water and I watched them tear it up while I slipped into my suit. Rohloff was perched on the lower deck of the lifeguard station and he asked me where I had been and I told him about my grandma's funeral. He nodded and changed the subject. As I zipped up I noticed Benji staring at me. He was sitting by the lone palm tree with a few of his buddies. I ignored his stare and Rohloff said that Benji was talking shit about how he was going to snake me.

Watch out, said Rohloff.

I shrugged and told myself that the only thing that mattered was to ride the waves and avoid the bullshit.

I'm just here to have fun, I said to Rohloff.

That's cool, said Rohloff.

I concentrated on the waves and how they were breaking and where I would take off and I ignored Benji's stinkeye. I strolled to the point and dropped onto my board, ducking under a little insider. A layer of sorrow wiped right off me and it seemed like I could see for a thousand miles. I sat with the legend pack on the point and they asked me where I had been. I told them.

You've had a rough go, said Shane.

I shrugged.

Norm, he said. Just hang in there. It'll turn around.

I nodded.

I surfed for an hour and it was hard to get waves with all the *heavy boyz* out. Finally Shane went in and that opened up a bit more space. I was eager to snag a set wave and I could feel the frustration darting inside me. Something menacing was rising up and it seemed like everything I had hoped to let go of was surging back and that made me desperate to burn it up. Suddenly I really wanted to shred a wave in front of Benji and his crew.

I heard somebody calling my name from the bluff. I squinted and recognized Nick's body language. He had one hand on his hip and the other waved me in.

Get your ass in here, Norman, he yelled.

I saw the crew on the beach turn from me to Nick then back to me.

Wanting to minimize the embarrassing drama I paddled right in.

Busted, said Benji with a smile when I passed him.

Most of the locals knew Nick from the old days and as I gathered my shorts, shirt and flip-flops they said things like *He looks agro. Tell Nick to take a 'lude.*

I meekly waved good-bye to the surf crew and hauled my gear up the dirt trail.

Nick had both hands on his hips when I reached the top.

Do you think we're all here to clean up your fucking messes? he said.

No, I said.

He jabbed his finger into my breastbone.

You do not exist at the center of the universe, he said, punctuating some words by jabbing harder.

I know, I said.

No you don't. You're a fucking self-centered thankless little shit.

I shook my head.

No I'm not, I said.

Yes you are, Norman. Yes you are.

What did I do? I yelled at him.

You left Sunshine out.

Oh shit. Is she okay?

That's beside the point. The point is she could be dead by now. Eaten alive by those fucking coyotes. You don't give a shit about her or about anything but yourself.

That's not true, I said.

Yes it is.

No it's not. I just got so stoked that I forgot.

That's a bullshit excuse, Norman.

He pressed his nose against my nose. The whites of his eyes were mucus yellow. I recognized that he wanted to hit me and punish me and make me squirm. In that moment I envisioned myself much older and I was screaming and hell-bent, fighting a bunch of angry faces, eager to punish them like Nick wanted to punish me. When I came out of this vision and saw him again I was merely fascinated by his rage. What else could Nick do but fight all those demons, I thought, and try to slay them before they sucked him into their darkness?

I slapped his finger off my chest and stepped back. He snickered at my retreat.

I never want to become you, I declared to myself.

Tears welled from a hot cavern in my chest and washed him out of sight. I moved away and followed my feet. When I looked up I was walking along the bluff away from the point toward the bus stop. I held my board tight to my ribs and I cried and watched the waves roll into the cove. I wanted to dive into those long bending swells. As I imagined my escape the rage and pain converged with the shimmering light blooming off the water. It all blended into one, like rivers entwining. This invisible current swept me up and it felt right to go with it.

I ran down the embankment and across the horseshoed sand in the cove. The beach was empty and smelled like seaweed. I dropped my board and streaked for the ocean. When I hit the water my skin stung as if cakes of dried mud were tearing off of me. Now there was nothing buffering me from the pain.

I miss you, Dad.

I felt my tears flooding into the water. I opened my eyes. It was murky down there. A big shit storm.

You vanished.

I dove deeper and skimmed the sandy bottom. Dark.

You left me all alone. All alone.

I needed air. Surfaced. The ocean under my chin rippled and swayed. I was not *okay* like I wanted to believe. I was sad. I was angry. And it made me feel ugly and lonely and cruel sometimes.

I came to shore and pounded the sand with my fists. I kicked and beat the sand for a long time. When I was worn out I rolled onto my side and stared at the ocean.

I was in pieces. Unable to gather myself back together. I stopped trying, and it wasn't so bad to be in pieces. I was calm, easy, light. Then the pain cut deeper into me, all over me. But somehow it was all right to feel things so close to my bones. The pain did not crush me.

The ocean spread out and the swells undulated and the waves looked beautiful peeling down the point. Dad taught me to fly right there on those waves. They were there for me to ride for all time, like the powder, streaming through the center of my body. I stood up.

The sand filled out the high arches of my feet, balancing me. In the hiss of the surf whispered my dad, asking me to trust that heaving wave in Mexico, trust that the ominous wall would bend and wrap me in its peaceful womb, revealing everything essential, a dream world of pure happiness—*beyond all the bullshit*.

Off the point at Topanga Beach I stared into the eye of a distant wave. Somewhere in the oval opening I grasped what Dad had always tried to make me see. There is more to life than just surviving it. Inside each turbulence there is a calm—a sliver of light buried in the darkness.

EPILOGUE

TWENTY-SEVEN YEARS LATER, I was driving to Mammoth with my six-year-old son, Noah, and we pulled into Lone Pine. As always, I pointed out Mount Whitney. It was haloed by swirls of snow dust alone in the bluest of sky. Noah was playing his Game Boy and he glanced at the blocky summit, yawned, then suddenly asked,

Did your dad use to show you Mount Whitney too on the way to Mammoth?

Yep, I said.

Is it true that you skied the Cornice when you were four?

Yep.

But you're not going to make me ski it. Right? he said.

No. Those were different times. My dad made me do lots of things that I'd get arrested for making you do.

Really? he said.

Oh yeah, I said.

Like what?

By the time we reached Bishop I had chronicled our skiing exploits from L.A. to Utah, and Noah had stowed his Game Boy in the backseat cubbyhole.

Noah asked me lots of questions and I answered them the best I could. Then as we climbed the Sherwin Grade out of Bishop he asked me about the airplane crash. I paused. He knew the general facts, his curiosity piqued by the scar on my chin. Now it was time to reveal more details, leaving out the goriest parts. I wanted to demystify the ordeal so that he would understand that reaching deep into yourself to overcome something seemingly indomitable was accessible to everyone, especially him.

Forty minutes later our car skidded and lurched in the snow along the road to our old cabin. It was snowing hard. I pulled into the driveway, stopped and looked in the rearview. Noah was staring at the back of my head, eyes narrowed, mulling over the ordeal I had just laid bare for him.

That's the story, I said.

Were you scared? he said.

Yeah, but I was in shock, I said. I just focused on getting down. There was no time to be scared.

I opened the door and then his door and he stepped out into the fresh powder. We looked at each other and I saw that he was okay, eyes bright and strong. He kicked the snow with his boot and the crystals spread wide, floating.

Should be some good powder skiing tomorrow, he said, parroting my enthusiasm.

Yep, I said. If you have any questions it's okay to ask them. You can ask me anything. Okay?

I know, he said.

.   .   .

I had always wondered what exactly went wrong during our flight back in 1979. It took me twenty-seven years to get up the guts to find out. I obtained the National Transportation Safety Board's Accident Report for our *incident*. The verbatim transmissions between the pilot and the control towers were included in the report.

Once I had it in hand I met my friend Michael Entin at the Santa Monica Airport. Michael has over twenty-five years of flying experience. When I sat down in the front seat of his four-seat Cessna and saw all those switches and dials, and the radar tower out the windshield, my throat went sticky and my heart beat against my breastbone. The sky was blue, yet I felt dreary, as if it were overcast all of a sudden.

You were doomed from takeoff, said Michael right away.

He pointed to one of Rob's first transmissions: *I'm, ah, VFR* [Visual Flight Rules] *over, ah, LA en route to Big Bear airport for landing, I'd like, ah, radar following for a steer, unfamiliar with the area.*

Thirty seconds into your flight Rob was already lost and had no idea where he was going, said Michael. He was using an underpowered plane with no instruments on a cloudy day—he never should have taken off, much less proceeded toward the storm ahead.

Apparently, air traffic control warned Rob three times during our flight not to fly VFR—meaning the pilot can see for at least two miles in all directions and there are no foreseeable obstructions to his maintaining this ability.

Worse, said Michael, it says here that the pilot never even got a weather briefing or filed a flight plan. Basic stuff, Norm. Had he done that, he would have known not to take off.

What a waste, I thought. My father wasn't killed by an avalanche while skiing an epic powder bowl. No giant tube ate him alive at the moment of ecstasy. Instead, a guy he didn't know took him on a doomed, easily avoidable airplane ride, killing him, his girlfriend and almost his son.

When we had finished poring over the transmissions I was nauseous and wanted out of the plane. Michael was studying the NTSB tracking map of our 1979 flight path, and I searched for the door handle.

You want to retrace the flight? said Michael, and my hand froze on the lever. Figure out where Rob went off course?

I looked out the window—not one cloud in the sky. I took a deep breath. This is a once-in-a-lifetime opportunity, I told myself.

Then my stomach lurched into my throat. No fucking way, I thought.

Yeah, that'd be great. Let's go for it, I said.

Michael fired up the turboprop, went through his checklist, and I settled into the passenger seat, slipping on the headphones just as I had when I was eleven years old.

We retraced the 1979 flight path, wandering off course up San Antonio Canyon, swooping over Ontario Peak. It made me woozy but I wouldn't get another chance at this, so I took it all in.

Then Michael flew us over the Big Bear airport. The landing strip, tucked into the mountains at nearly seven thousand feet, cut a black swath in the tall evergreens and butted up against Big Bear Lake.

It's an unmanned airport, he said. There's no one down there to guide you in—you're on your own. If Rob had filed a flight plan and weather briefing he would have known that he was flying into a socked-in airport. Even with my turbo power and all these sophisticated instruments I wouldn't have tried to land there on that day. No way.

. . .

The first thing that struck me when dawn broke and I stepped out of my car and stood facing Ontario Peak looming over me was how unfriendly the terrain was. It was a clear September day in 2006 and I was wandering around the foot of Icehouse Canyon Trail, just above Baldy Village, contemplating how to climb up to the place near the top of Ontario Peak where I thought perhaps our plane had crashed. By chance a woman named Katie was starting up the trail on her morning hike, and I asked her if she knew the Chapmans.

Fifteen minutes later I was sitting next to Pat Chapman in the same rocking chair, warming my hands by the same pot-belly stove, as I had twenty-seven years before. We had some hot chocolate and recounted the events of February 19, 1979.

Pat was awakened that morning by a loud thud. Her first thought was that it sounded like a plane crashing. Then a coyote kept howling and she remembers a strange beeping noise. She didn't say anything to her husband Bob because she just wasn't sure of what she had heard.

Later that morning, nagged by a remote yet unshakable feeling that something bad had happened on the mountain, she led her two sons on a miserable hike to the meadow. They called out toward Ontario Peak, above the crown of rock, into the long apron that she called Gooseberry Canyon. Although the canyon was several thousand feet away, their voices echoed off the canyon walls. The wind and heavy fog buffered their voices some that day. When no one answered, she figured that her hunch was wrong.

Pat told me that not long after she had safely delivered me to the detective, a sheriff's deputy came to her door and asked for a statement. Pat recounted the day for him. How she had been awakened by a noise that sounded like a plane crashing into the mountain, and how she later climbed to the meadow. When she finished her account, the deputy informed her that she could not have heard a plane and that it must have been the snowplow clearing the highway.

I didn't respond, she told me. Some things are not easily explained.

Eventually I got in touch with Glenn Farmer, the teenager who I ran into on the dirt road. I think we were both shocked to hear each other's voices—we hadn't seen or heard from each other since that day twenty-seven years ago when Glenn carried me in his arms to the Chapman Ranch. We talked on the phone for an hour. He was a wealth of information, and finally I asked him why he was on that dirt road in such nasty weather, yelling out.

Glenn explained what led him there on February 19, 1979. At around 2:30 p.m. he had spoken to some sheriff Search and Rescue guys outside the burger joint, a few hundred yards from the entrance to the Chapman ranch. The rescue guys were pointing up at Ontario Peak, talking about how long it would take them to hike up there. He asked them what was wrong and they said a plane had crashed. Because it was so foggy, hiding Ontario Peak from view, Glenn mistakenly believed that they were pointing at the crown of rock—the backside of the massive ridgeline— thousands of feet lower.

So when Search and Rescue drove away, Glenn decided to hike up toward that lower crown of rock and see what he could find. He was never able to get close to the crown because the buckthorn was too thick. Glenn said he had yelled many times and, having given up, was walking back down the dirt road when he decided to give it one more shot.

. . .

A month after my first meeting with Pat Chapman, I met up with her son Evan Chapman for a guided tour back up the mountain. He led me across the meadow, tunneling us through the buck-thorn, with no snow traps to worry about this time, and we scratched up the waterfall of rock—iceless—and up the gulch and the long apron, right to where I had found Sandra—he knew the exact place because his father, the late Bob Chapman, had pointed it out.

After locating the area where Sandra had ended her violent fall, he left me alone for a few minutes. I told Sandra I was sorry she didn't make it, that I was sorry I blew it and miscal-culated her slide path. Then Evan led me across the enclave of trees and we found the frame of the seat that had slid down to the same area.

At 7,300 feet I thanked Evan for his guidance. He handed me a walkie-talkie and pointed me toward the infamous chute, one of three that forked up to Ontario Peak.

When I came upon a seam of pure dirt that cut down one side of the chute, free of shale, I knew that, when covered with snow, it became the brutally slick funnel. I had to crouch onto all fours to follow it upward. About an hour later I recognized a tree. It was the tallest amongst a line of them, rare within the chute. It was so steep that even without ice I had to lean my shoulder into the hill in order to look across the chute and study the tree. My gut told me it was the tree that had supported the wing, our shelter.

Tired, sweaty and dusty, I sat on a flat rock where I figured the impact zone was in relation to the tree. Right away I began reliving my time here twenty-seven years before in the snow and wind. After a while I was finally able to focus on my dad.

Although I had no hard evidence, I believed that this was where his magnificent life had been snatched away.

Well Dad, this is where it all ended, I said aloud. Thanks for protecting me. I wish I could have saved you.

I felt him like a steam rising out of the mountain. I let him seep in. Tears spilled and I moaned and I wondered if the bears or the coyotes heard me. I drifted there, savoring everything we had accomplished together, so fantastic and grueling.

Cautiously I rotated and lowered and kissed the rock, the general area where he had died. When I opened my eyes there was something orange and white under a crushed pinecone, wedged between smaller pieces of shale. I dug it out. A carbon fiber shard as big as my hand, the orange paint dull and mealy. I dug more and found two more pieces much like it. Our plane had been orange, red, and white. The tire housing and other mostly superficial parts of the plane were made of carbon fiber. I turned the pieces over, marveling at the discovery, then kissed the rocks and the pinecone and told my dad how much I loved him again.

I looked out over the long apron, known as Gooseberry Canyon, and through the gulch, searching for the meadow—my true north. But I could not find it. I knew where it was, I had walked through it four hours earlier, but I could not see it over the massive ridgeline rising from the gulch and blocking anything to the left of the gulch. I was perplexed.

Adding to the mystery, when I returned home I discovered an audiotape recorded from a TV interview that took place the day after the crash, February 20, 1979, and on it I say, *There was a meadow and I tried to go toward that every time because I knew there was a house near there*. Yet from my highest vantage point on this clear October day in 2006 I was not able to see the meadow and failed to spot it during my descent that afternoon. It was eclipsed by the ridgeline and only visible once I made it through the gulch. I checked my photographs taken from that high vantage point in the chute, and there is no mistake. The meadow is not visible. Only the rooftop is visible from the chute—it sits right in the sightline of the gulch. The overgrown dirt road cutting up from the rooftop is visible too. But not the meadow—it's too far left, hidden behind the ridgeline.

I had always believed that I had spotted the meadow, the rooftop and the dirt road just after the helicopter flew away, and that *I tried to go toward that meadow every time because I knew there was a house near there*. And even in the face of insurmountable contradictory evidence I still have a vivid memory of heading toward that meadow, compelled to reach it, believing that it would guide me to safety.

Bears and wolves navigate wilderness by instinct, and migratory birds are guided by an internal compass, so maybe the notion that I had to see the meadow in order for me to perceive it is an artificial concept.

Maybe I sensed a place where I could rest from the steep ice and broken terrain—a place where other humans like Pat were compelled to go—just as a wolf or bear can sense such places. Maybe the footprints of Pat and her boys, those human markings, called to me, and because I was cut off from civilization I was able to access my animal instinct and hang on to life.

When Noah was born I was concerned that he would grow up feeling the same pressure to be a great surfer and skier that I had felt. I prepared myself for the genetic code to kick in, directing me to push my son as I had been pushed.

Often I've wondered why my father was so compelled to drive

me the way he did. Was it to make me in his image? To compensate for his own unfulfilled wishes? Probably both, I figured.

I don't know if my father was right or wrong to raise me the way he did. It does seem reckless. But when I delve into those memories, extracting the details, it doesn't *feel* reckless. It feels like life as I know it. Raw and wild and wonderfully unpredictable. Perhaps my reaction can be explained as mere conditioning—my father conditioned me to feel comfortable in the storm.

This by no means is to suggest that I breeze through life. I stumble and claw my way through like most of us. With my crude tools and imperfect skills I make my way through the chaos with the hope that I will find a little piece of beauty buried in it.

With this on my mind as I raise my own son, I often think about how much and how often I should impose my passions on Noah's budding interests. I don't want my relationship with Noah to be a continuation of my relationship with my father, or to be used selfishly to heal my wounds. Yet I feel obligated to expose Noah to my father's passionate nature, his ability to live life to the fullest. Managing these opposing forces has always been a difficult balance.

The first time I took Noah skiing, he was four years old. By the time I was four I had already carved up most of the black diamonds in Mammoth, and I knew it was imperative that I resist the impulse to push Noah to do the same. Miraculously, I was able to locate a deeply buried streak of patience within, and Noah was awarded with the luxury of getting to go at his own pace.

I had it under control until he was seven. Noah had just skied

Dave's Run, a formidable black diamond, and I was so elated that I led him on a long traverse under the Dragon's Back. Along the way, the narrow path became littered with rocks and half-buried tree limbs. I casually skied beneath him in case he hit one and got pitched off the traverse.

We were nearly there, a protected gully that I guessed would have soft snow, allowing Noah to carve his turns even though it was steep. As we traversed the last twenty feet, approaching the rim of the gully, which curved away like a sheet of water draping over the edge of a waterfall, the snow turned to ice. Noah's skis chattered and he lost elevation quickly. I encouraged him to bear down and crank his edges into the ice. But his legs were wobbling with fear and he began to cry. I got below him and coaxed him toward the rim. I'll catch you, I said. Just try it. Reluctantly, he squatted and angled into the hill. We swooped onto the rim.

Noah stopped on the lip of the rim, staring down into the gully. It was steeper than I had remembered it. Though, down in its heart, the snow was soft.

No way, Dad, said Noah, plopping down on his hip. I can't do that.

Of course you can, I said. See how the snow is soft in there. With your great technique it'll be easy to hold an edge. Easier than this ice.

You shouldn't have taken me here, was his response.

Well, we're here now, I said.

I had a pretty good idea of how Noah felt hovering over the lip of the gully. Having been in similar situations at nearly the same age, I understood that he just didn't want to be scared, didn't want to feel all that tension in his body, no matter what the payoff might be. He wanted to have effortless fun.

The essence of my conflict, and I believe the essence of the conflict for my father, was illuminated in this moment. In the gully awaited fresh, protected snow—a little treasure secreted away from the sun and wind by its north-facing hemmed-in design. The supple snow in this gully would allow Noah to feel the rush of g-forces pulling against his defiant arc—the full extent of which would not be possible with anything but fresh snow. He would feel the sensation of banking on a thin rail along the mightiest current of all—gravity—an act of supreme freedom. Not to mention the feeling of empowerment that would follow. But he had to fight through the fear, the daunting lip and crusty sidewall, to capture that moment. Left to his own devices, I thought, it might take years for Noah to tackle his fear. For my father, and sometimes for me, this waste was too much for us to bear—the boy must taste the thrill now!

I'm stuck, said Noah. This sucks.

I could lift him in my arms and carry him down into the gully, I contemplated. Then my old dad got the better of me, piping up—You can do it, Noah. You're golden. Accordingly I dropped into the gully. It was steep and the icy contours knobbing the sidewall were like a gauntlet, kicking and bucking my skis until I hit the soft snow. Now Noah would have to drop in too.

Like the onset of an itch, I sensed that I had crossed the line, and that I was suddenly caught up in my own selfish drama. On the other hand, the situation was contained: I was right there to catch him if he tumbled into the gully, and the snow was soft where he would land. I stuck with the plan and waited for Noah to make a move.

The plan backfired. Noah began writhing and bawling uncontrollably.

I was looking up at him from the heart of the gully and I

thought I might have to attempt to sidestep the precipitous, crusty sidewall and rescue him.

What am I going to do? he screamed down at me.

You can ski that ice along the edge of the gully, or you can ski this soft fluff down here, I said. Your choice.

I pretended that this was really some kind of a choice.

His little head moved to the left, then back to the right. Then all of a sudden he stood up and dropped over the lip. His whole body chattered as he careened down the crusty sidewall. When his skis hit the soft snow his body relaxed in an instant.

Keep it going, Ollestad, I said as he swished across the fall line, gathering courage to make the dreaded first turn.

He shifted his weight, committed his skis and shoulders down the pitch, and made a beautiful turn. Then another. He really had to lean into the hill because it was so steep, and I thought about the soft snow cradling him if he fell, dampering his slide, giving me time to scoop him up.

I yelled for him to stop at the tree line. But he ignored me and disappeared in the woods below. I found him at the chairlift and skied up beside him, expecting a blast of anger. Maybe his experience was not as elating as I had anticipated. Maybe he hated every second of it.

What took you so long? he said, full of gusto.

It was steep, I said.

Good snow though, he said.

We loaded onto Chair 9, the only way out of this back corner of the resort. On the ride up we did not speak. He rested his head against my upper arm. I knew I had gone too far. I knew that we were both lucky it worked out. I also knew that he had found a formerly unknown well of confidence, and that he could draw on this in all areas of his life. There were certainly more graceful ways to reach this same end. I just didn't know them like I knew this. So my struggle for the right balance of free will and force continues.

We neared the top of the chairlift. I glanced at Noah. He was staring across the giant sail-shaped bowl, pondering the gully in the distance.

How's it feel? I said.

He just nodded and kept staring at it. I guessed that at some point during his run, Noah had broken through the storm and locked into the bliss of his victory, the bliss of his connection to the ineffable—that sacred place unveiled to me, and now to my son, by the man with the sunshine in his eyes. There are few joys in life that can compare to that.

And then I reined myself back and asked him where he wanted to go next.

Lunch, he said.

Great idea, Ollestad.

ACKNOWLEDGMENTS

I am grateful to the following people for their invaluable contributions to this book.

(In alphabetical order)

Lloyd Ahern, Kevin Anderson, Rachel Bressler, Bob Chapman, Evan Chapman, Patricia Chapman, Michael Entin, John Evans, Glenn Farmer, Jenny Frank, Alan Freedman, Sue Freedman, Harvey Good, Dan Halpern, Dave Kitching, Eleanor Kendall, Lee Kendall, George McCormick, Doris Ollestad, Noah Ollestad, David Rapkin, Craig Rosenberg, Carolyn See, Virginia Smith, Fonda Snyder, Rob Weisbach, Gary Wilson.

About the Author

About the Book

Insights,
Interviews
& More . . .

Read On

Meet Norman Ollestad

JULES REVELLE

NORMAN OLLESTAD studied creative writing at UCLA and attended UCLA Film School. He grew up on Topanga Beach in Malibu and now lives in Venice, California. He is the father of a nine-year-old son. ᕼ

Q&A with the Author

This Q&A originally appeared on www.bookreporter.com in June 2009.

The events in Crazy for the Storm happened more than thirty years ago. Did you always know that you wanted to write about them? If not, what motivated you to write this memoir now?

When I was twenty-one, ski-bumming in Europe, I realized that I wanted to be a writer. The deeper I got into that state of mind, the more I understood that I would write the story of my father and myself, our crash, our life together. Then I sort of forgot about it, until my then-six-year-old son began to remind me of myself when I was young—my son and I were doing the same things that I did with my dad, surfing and skiing together. On a long drive to Mammoth Ski Resort, I recounted to my son the crash and some of my adventures with my father. When I finished the story my son said, "You have to make that into a book"—and so I did.

Tell us a little about the experience of writing the memoir. Were there any ▶

> "On a long drive to Mammoth Ski Resort, I recounted to my son the crash and some of my adventures with my father. When I finished the story my son said, 'You have to make that into a book.'"

3

emotions or reactions that came up during the writing process that surprised you?

I often got sore throats after a day of writing. I had to sleep a lot. My body was lethargic but I forced myself to exercise, to keep my body and mind alert. Writing the book made me really appreciate how devoted my father was to me.

How about the actual events? Has everything remained as vivid in your own memory for the past thirty years as it comes across in your writing, or did you need to return to some locations to research and explore them again to fill in pieces?

Returning to the locations, especially Baldy, helped link my scattered memories together, and the geography instigated a lot of buried memories—I have always had a strong geographical memory, so seeing those trees and rocks and touching the terrain again was very helpful. Then retracing the flight really brought it all home. I interviewed family, friends, and witnesses, and reviewed the NTSB report, sheriff's report, and news clips to fill in some of the gaps, or reinforce my recollections.

Tell us what it was like to grow up on Topanga Beach in Malibu in the heart of the 1970s. Is there any place like it now, or was that something that existed only in that time and place?

There has never been anything quite like it, and I don't think there ever will be again. It was a blend of many diverse types of people, all living together in a small cove, a tainted paradise, in a time of great upheaval and freedom.

Reading about life on Topanga Beach is not at all what we would picture as the world where an ex–FBI agent would live. FBI implies life with rules while Topanga was open and free. What did your dad do with the FBI? What were his impressions of his time there? And why did he leave?

My father left the FBI because Hoover was corrupt and hypocritical. My father liked to swim in many different social oceans—he sought out the unknown, loved to explore new environments, and Topanga Beach was a quintessentially spontaneous and unpredictable place, so he was attracted to it. ▶

66 There has never been anything quite like it [Topanga Beach in the 1970s], and I don't think there ever will be again. It was a blend of many diverse types of people, all living together in a small cove, a tainted paradise, in a time of great upheaval and freedom. 99

In some of the sections that take place both before and after the crash, you seem to contrast the ways your dad pushed you to be brave, to challenge yourself, with the very different ways your mom's boyfriend tried to control your behavior. What characteristics do you think go into being a good dad?

Show your child that you are interested in them, devoted to them. Share your passions. Keep exposing them to what you believe will fulfill them. Then let them decide whether or not they want to indulge. And don't be afraid to make mistakes— everybody can learn from mistakes— just try not to repeat them.

You have an eight-year-old son. What kinds of activities do you do together? How would you characterize your relationship?

We do a lot of homework together. We surf and ski as much as we can. I believe my son knows that I am devoted to him. He's not afraid to tell me how he feels about something I may be doing that he doesn't like, and I allow him to speak his mind. But I'm still the head gorilla.

Near the end of the memoir, you return to the crash site for the first time since February 1979. What was it like to return to that spot? Have your thoughts about your dad evolved as you became a father yourself?

Writing the book has made me realize how devoted my father was to me—he instilled an attitude that has always enabled me to find the beauty in life, even when it seemed impossible to uncover. I'm impressed by his passion for life, his optimistic point of view. I try to pass that on to my son.

In the scenes that take place during the crash, you make it clear that the lessons your dad taught you directly or indirectly saved your life on the mountainside. In the years since, do you still feel your dad's lessons have been useful to you in other situations?

Yes. In many ways his lessons have been even more useful in navigating what I call "regular life." Which is more complicated because life does not have laws that it follows like Nature does.

One of the most striking things about the narration is the shift between the harrowing events on the mountain and earlier events, including the ▶

> ❝ [My father's] lessons have been even more useful in navigating what I call 'regular life.' Which is more complicated because life does not have laws that it follows like Nature does. ❞

road trip to Mexico with your father, in alternating chapters. Did you always plan to organize the memoir this way? What do you hope fathers and sons will take away from your memoir?

I wrote a few drafts in chronological order, then realized it needed the juxtaposition to really come alive— that took a few days to organize.

Some reviewers have been calling your writing style "Hemingwayesque." What novelists and memoirists have influenced you the most?

Hemingway has always inspired me, and haunted me because of his seemingly effortless prose. Cutting to the bone is hard to do, but, I believe, easier and more fulfilling to read. There are so many great writers that I learn from that it's impossible to list; however, Cormac McCarthy is certainly a writer I hold in the highest regard, as well as Jhumpa Lahiri.

Do you plan to do more writing? What else would you like to, or do you plan to, write about?

Yes. I am a writer for life. I'm sketching out my next book and

hope to get it underway in the fall.
I can envision my next two books,
and some short story/novellas I'd
like to take a crack at. Meanwhile
I'm doing some pieces for *Men's
Journal* and other publications. ∿

Reading Group Guide
Questions for discussion

Introduction

From the age of three, Norman Ollestad was thrust into the world of surfing and competitive downhill skiing by the intense, charismatic father he both idolized and resented. While his friends were riding bikes, playing ball, and going to birthday parties, young Norman was whisked away in pursuit of wild and demanding adventures. Yet it was this kind of exhilarating test of skill that prepared "Boy Wonder," as his father called him, to become a fearless champion—and ultimately saved his life.

Questions for Discussion

1. Discuss the various ways to interpret the book's title, *Crazy for the Storm*. How did this perspective/attitude shape young Norman's personality and life? Did it help save his life?

2. Was Norman's father too demanding of his son? How has parenting changed since the era of the book, the 1970s? How is the father-son relationship like or unlike your own relationship with your own father?

3. On that fateful day of the crash, little Norman was forced to draw from all the tools and lessons his father had instilled in him from birth. Discuss the connections between what his father exposed him to and when he had to put those experiences to quick use on the mountain.

4. Have you been faced with a seemingly insurmountable situation that forced you to reach deep down inside yourself in order to make it through?

5. What sports, activities, or hobbies give you the most satisfaction? Discuss the role your favorite sport, activity, or hobby plays in your life. Could you cope without it?

6. Have you had early childhood experiences forced upon you that at first you resisted and rejected, but that later became a most favored or treasured experience, skill, or pastime?

7. Empowering messages were ingrained in Norman, the "Boy Wonder," from an early age, such as "Never give up" and "We can do it all." These words fueled Norman to keep moving forward each time he weakened or seemed about to succumb. What words and thoughts wield significant power to you?

8. How does the tone from the beginning of the book compare ▶

to the end? Does Norman seem to have reconciled the tension generated by his father's insistence to push beyond the limits of the comfort zone? At the conclusion of the book, is the author softened, resolved, or conflicted?

9. In contrast to his father's risk-taking nature, young Norman seemed to possess an inherent sense of reserve and caution. Throughout the story, when do we see Norman first begin to emerge from his fears and begin to embrace the joy of the thrill-seeking his father craved?

10. There were a few important women who influenced Norman early in his life, including Patricia Chapman, who provided the warm, safe haven when he finally made it down the mountain. How did each relationship impact him and shape him? Did they offer a counterbalance to the dominant male personalities in his life?

Q&A with the Author *(continued)*

Q&A with the Author *(continued)*

Don't miss the next book by your favorite author. Sign up now for AuthorTracker by visiting www.AuthorTracker.com.